UNIQUE EATS AND EATERIES

OF

NEW ORLEANS

ELIZABETH M. WILLIAMS

CONTENTS

INTRODUCTION

The city of New Orleans is at once mired in tradition and embracing new flavors and ideas. Tradition is an important part of the city's identity, and that includes traditions surrounding food and drink. Those tentacles of tradition seem to embrace all New Orleanians. Not every city faces a catastrophe that actually threatens its existence, but New Orleans did, in August 2005, when Hurricane Katrina caused a flood that covered 80% to 85% of the city. The city was evacuated and people were scattered all over the country.

At that time, the Southern Food & Beverage Museum was not yet open, but it had a website. During the weeks and even months that people lived outside the city, they began to search for their comfort foods. When they could not find filé in the grocery stores, or coffee and chicory, or proper beans, they wrote to the Southern Food & Beverage Museum asking for help in finding these basic ingredients. The foods that could be made represented an important part of the city's and its people's identity. Being able to make gumbo comforted them. It allowed them to remain New Orleanians.

As people came back to the city and began to rebuild their homes and re-establish the life of the city, they found ruined homes with ruined kitchens. So they began to eat in restaurants. Those restaurants opened before their owners even fixed their own homes. And it was the restorative power of the restaurants that gave the people not only hope in the form of a functioning city, but hope in the return of their identity.

While New Orleans was and is a truly American city, complete with fast food establishments and chain restaurants, many of those places did not reopen in the aftermath of Hurricane Katrina. The demographics were wrong for reopening. But while the big chains did not return, the mom-and-pop restaurants did. The po'boy shops, the corner restaurants, and the old line restaurants did not wait for demographics to be correct for rebuilding. And the people returned the favor by eating out and sharing their experiences with their neighbors.

And the food continued to evolve into the exciting style we find today. Today we celebrate not only the early days of the city, the mid-nineteenth-century restaurants, and the turn-of-the-twentieth-century changes, today we look ahead to new flavors, twists on tradition, and old-fashioned ways. We eat at night, we eat with our hands, we dress up so much that many tourists are surprised, and we drink in the streets.

One of the most important aspects of the food of New Orleans is that everyone in the city eats the same food, everyone recognizes it, and everyone cooks it. This book does not introduce you to every restaurant in the city. But it does give you a taste of its diversity. Whether eating at a diner or eating at a white tablecloth restaurant, the taste of New Orleans is an entré into the identity of the city.

UNIQUE EATS AND EATERIES
OF
NEW ORLEANS

JACQUES-IMO'S

A creative kitchen in a creative space

A restaurant as imaginative as Jacques-Imo's is naturally the brainchild of an equally fascinating chef. You wouldn't think a Coast Guard Academy graduate from upstate New York would bring the kind of Cajun zeal that Chef Jacque Leonardi infuses into every dish, but then again you also might not think you want alligator in your cheesecake. And you definitely do.

Jacques-Imo's is a restaurant that can best be described as, "eclectic New Orleans." It feels like a neighborhood place in some respects, especially if you sit at the bar. But people from all over the city come to eat there, either with out-of-town guests or alone. It's funky enough to show off as a piece of New Orleans charm, but good enough to satisfy the need for a taste of New Orleans.

Jacques Leonardi cooked under the great Paul Prudhomme, learning not only how to cook, but how to think about a restaurant. Leonardi opened Jacques-Imo's in the 1990s and has established a quirky restaurant with idiosyncratic decorations which attracts so many patrons that people have been known to wait hours happily for a table. Leonardi absorbed Chef Paul's techniques of layering flavor. The food is extraordinarily creative and the lines attest to how much New Orleanians appreciate it.

Besides Prudhomme, Leonardi worked with Chef Austin Leslie of Chez Hélène fame. From Chef Austin, Leonardi learned the secret of fried chicken. Now that he's perfected it at Jacques-Imo's, you should eat some there. The eggplant with oyster dressing shows its Prudhomme roots. On the other hand, the alligator and shrimp

> Chef Austin Leslie was a talented character. He was known for his fried chicken and for wearing a captain's hat. He was the model for the television show, *Frank's Place*, starring Tim Reid.

Left: Jambalaya.
Right: Intimate seating.

cheesecake is all Leonardi's own creation. It's wildly eclectic with snails, rabbit, chicken livers, and calamari, and it's wildly popular with guests, too. The paneed rabbit with tasso pasta is another favorite.

Jacques-Imo's is known for its huge portions and really interesting, tasty food. It's also known for being so popular that you spend a long time waiting for a table—easily up to two hours any night of the week. You can usually avoid or at least minimize this problem by deciding to eat at eccentric times. And when you arrive knowing that the wait is ahead of you, just accept it and start drinking with the other waiting guests. Quite a few friendships have been formed waiting for a table at Jacques-Imo's.

One of the highlights of the restaurant is that it doesn't hold back on flavor. Steak with blue cheese, butter, and cream sauces just enrich everything and make it all better. The wine list is short, but interesting. It'll hold up to the food. There are also local beers and non-alcoholic drinks available. Once your table is finally ready you'll get to walk through the kitchen on the way to your seat. Unconventional to be sure, but the aromas will only heighten your anticipation of the great meal that awaits.

8324 Oak St.
New Orleans, LA
504-861-0886
jacques-imos.com

BETWEEN THE BREAD

An unexpected place for breakfast or a sandwich

As a sister restaurant to Café at the Square, these two Smith-and-Hary–owned restaurants are doing the lion's share of the work to feed hungry downtown visitors first thing in the morning. In a city with many famous breakfast choices, it's good to know which ones are consistently reliable. Between the Bread is a place to eat breakfast that's open early and that serves good food. It's located on St. Charles Avenue in the middle of the Central Business District. There are many hotels nearby, as well as condos and offices. It's the place of choice for many regulars who go for the tasty food, signature dishes, and reliable service.

David Smith and Doug Hary, founders, opened the restaurant to serve downtown offices in a post–Hurricane Katrina wasteland. And they did so with American sandwiches on dense, delicious bread and with freshly cooked meats. The restaurant has grown into the favorite and most dependable place for many office workers in the downtown area.

For breakfast you can go light, with seasonal fruit or granola that is house made, or you can go heavy, with a pressed bacon, cheese, and tomato sandwich. Try a peanut butter and jelly pressed sandwich with banana and Nutella. Bagels with salmon and cream cheese or other breakfast sandwiches are available.

If you're preparing for a picnic, this is the place to pick up fresh chicken salad, egg salad, tuna salad, and pimento cheese. There's also pasta salad and potato salad. Buy bread and make your own sandwiches.

Lunch in the restaurant consists of the classic sandwiches and sides. There are salads, like the olive and Parmesan pasta salad or the garden salad. There's an Asian salad with chow mein noodles that can be made with chicken, smoked salmon, or turkey. The meat and blue salad is

Cobb salad and assorted sandwiches.

made with roast beef, blue cheese, and mixed greens. There is a soup of the day, but the main lunch offerings are sandwiches for you to embellish with bacon, extra cheese, extra meat, and chips.

The Reuben is made with corned beef, sauerkraut, and cheese. Hot pastrami with cheese is another favorite choice. The chicken pesto sandwich is made with sliced chicken and pesto. A club sandwich is available as well as a veggie sandwich. Between the Bread closes in the afternoon, but is one of those faithful standbys when you need a portable meal that is tasty and filling.

625 St. Charles Ave.
New Orleans, LA
504-324-5304
betweenthebreadnola.com

CARROLLTON MARKET

An Uptown restaurant with a special touch

The road to becoming a successful chef looks a little different for everyone. In the case of Carrollton Market's Chef Jason Goodenough, it looks like consistent hard work with a laser focus on perfecting the craft. His upbringing gave him an international palate. His formal training at the Culinary Institute of America gave him the fundamentals, and his apprenticeships under the likes of Georges Perrier and Emeril Lagasse gave him the confidence to strike out on his own when his moment came. Now, the fruits of all this labor are available to all at Carrollton Market.

Named for a nineteenth century public market that once stood near the restaurant, Carrollton Market has been turning heads since its doors opened in 2014. Chef Jason Goodenough wants the food to be excellent, but also wants to be a responsible user of those sources of food so that they can be sustained over time. The future without good food and good sources of food is not a pretty one. Chef Goodenough provides an excellent menu full of grounded courses, which consistently exceeds expectations. The restaurant is a pleasing combination of decor, food, and service.

Dinner appetizers set the tone for the meal to come. A cinnamon roll pain perdu that supports a seared foie gras with a Luxardo cherry gastrique is quite a luxurious appetizer. The piquillo pepper appetizer presents the peppers stuffed with crabmeat and cheese with crispy Brussels sprouts and smoked paprika. The sweet corn soup is served with shrimp. And oysters Goodenough are flash fried and served with bacon, leeks, and Bernaise sauce. And that's just the appetizers.

Entrées include pork belly with fried rice, an egg, and bok choy. A steak frites with a Bernaise sauce sits tantalizingly on the menu. Roasted fish with mashed potatoes beckons. The blackened redfish is served with crawfish bread pudding. How decadent.

Left: From the sidewalk. Credit: Whitney Richard.
Right: Plated fish.

The brunch menu includes house-made cinnamon rolls and a poutine made with hand-cut fries and cheese curds. There is French toast stuffed with Creole cream cheese and blueberries. There's a hamburger with cheese spread with bacon and onion jam. If you need a hearty brunch offering, the steak frites with egg is available with a petite steak. There are pancakes and also an omelet with vegetables.

The wine list has been chosen to pair with the menu, and the list changes as the food changes. The list of wines is international in scope and reflects a wide knowledge of what the world has to offer. The bar program contains interesting house cocktails and a bar that can also produce traditional cocktails.

Chef Goodenough was named Chef of the Year by *New Orleans* magazine in December 2017. His take on Southern and New Orleans classics is quite international. The presentation of the dishes is remarkable. All in all a top-notch experience—good enough for a celebration, but worthy of regular attendance.

8132 Hampson St.
New Orleans, LA
504-252-9928
carrolltonmarket.com

WILLA JEAN

Bread and chocolate for breakfast all day

Southern baking, particularly its pastry and iconic biscuits, is among the most mouthwatering and nostalgic of treats. When the craving strikes, little attention can be paid to the hour or whether it's breakfast, lunch, or dinner. It's simply "biscuit time."

There to soothe that craving is Willa Jean, a combination bakery and café. It excels in both categories. Somehow, getting up before the crack of dawn to make muffins, bread, cookies, and other pastries doesn't deter the hardworking staff from staying open and operating all day long. You'll find no break in the action here—Willa Jean is always open and always busy.

The restaurant is bright and airy with a homey but industrial look. It's a very smart look, which makes for a cozy experience despite a soaring ceiling and lots of glass. And no matter when you arrive, the aroma of fresh bread is both inviting and tempting.

The restaurant opened in 2015 on the ground floor of the Paramount Building in the Central Business District. The location was a stroke of genius, because there wasn't another bakery in sight. It was the brainchild of Kelly Fields who brought her desire for a pastry-forward restaurant to fruition. And that pastry-forward concept was brought to the details of the decor. Pendant lights are ensconced in whisks, and brown paper hangs from a roll to let you know about the bakery specials. This is not a low-carb haven; but for those looking for comfort, this is the place.

The breakfast snacks include grilled banana bread, granola, and artichoke dip. The full breakfasts are much more extensive. Avocado toast with poached egg, BBQ shrimp toast, a grain bowl with beans, and eggs and avocado are just a few examples from a tempting list of choices. The hangover bowl will definitely equip you for the day, with shortribs, grits, a poached egg, and garlic. And then, of course, there are the biscuits: fried chicken biscuits, biscuits with butter and jam, sausage biscuits, and very Southern gravy biscuits.

Willa Jean cornbread with Poirier's cane syrup. Credit: Rush Jagoe.

Lunch includes toasts, sandwiches, and salads, all of which reflect the underlying structure of the bakery, and all the food is freshly made. The warm buttered crab roll, the WJ burger, and the fried chicken sandwich are good Southern sandwiches. The hot oyster po'boy includes blue cheese ranch—too tempting to resist. The kale salad, the roasted beet salad, and the artichoke and oyster soup make the lunch menu very difficult to navigate—the choices are simply too compelling.

The dinner menu includes the lunch menu plus some large plates. The grilled skirt steak, the fried pork chop, and the seared drum should satisfy any appetite. A brunch menu is served on Saturday and Sunday. This restaurant, the expression of Chef Kelly Fields's bakery aesthetic, is named Willa Jean for her grandmother. Chef Fields was named the Breakfast Chef of the Year by the Extra Crispy website and has been recognized by many other publications. We are all waiting for a cookbook, which we hope will be full of her delicious secrets.

Naturally, because this is a bakery, the dessert menu is definitely worth discussion. It includes red velvet cake, which is huge and rich. The banana pudding is served with traditional vanilla wafers. And while you're at Willa Jean, don't forget to check out the cookies, the muffins, and all of the other choices. The house-made breads are sensational, and may be worth the trip even without eating a meal.

611 O'Keefe St.
New Orleans, LA
504-509-7334
willajean.com

ARNAUD'S

It's like a eating in another time . . .

One of the grand dame restaurants in the French Quarter, Arnaud's looks just like its turn of the twentieth century origins. It opened in 1918. It is a beautiful space graced with dark paneling, leaded and colored glass windows, brass ceiling fans, and held together with traditional black-and-white tile floors. The restaurant's beauty truly enhances the dining experience. Arnaud's is open for dinner and brunch on Sundays. It is worth the trip for a relaxing, traditional meal.

Arnaud's was first opened by Arnaud Cazenave, a wine merchant in New Orleans. He famously operated the restaurant through Prohibition, though he was arrested for continuing to sell alcohol. He was just plying his trade. It is said that he teased Owen Brennan for being too Irish to run a fine dining establishment, prodding Brennan to ultimately open Brennan's Restaurant. Upon his death in 1978, his daughter, Germaine Wells, took over the restaurant, but it was ultimately sold to another couple, Archie and Jane Casbarian. They renovated the restaurant and updated the menu. Multiple generations of the family are still running this very traditional and classical place.

Like the other old-line restaurants, the menu is heavily based on seafood, including Shrimp Arnaud, which the restaurant considers its signature dish. It's a traditional shrimp remoulade served with perfectly poached shrimp and a sauce that is good enough to be bottled—it is

While you are visiting Arnaud's, take a few minutes to walk around the Germaine Wells Collection exhibition. It displays the many gowns, capes, and tiaras worn by a late owner and daughter of the founder of Arnaud's. She was active in the pageantry of Mardi Gras, clearly evident in the number of times that she participated in balls. And she is well recognized as the founder and force behind the annual Easter Parade.

Oysters Arnaud.

actually available at the restaurant and at local grocery stores. In addition, some of the traditional offerings are turtle soup served with sherry, a plethora of oyster dishes, and frog legs. The restaurant offerings include quail, chicken, duck, and traditional meats alongside escargot and alligator sausage.

Arnaud's offers an authentic New Orleans meal in a restful setting, where the sense of lingering over your meal is a genuine reflection of an earlier time. And its bar, French 75, presided over by the award-winning bartender, Chris Hanna, specializes in perfectly made, craft cocktails. Try a French 75 while you're there. The bar menu includes very elegant bar snacks such as savory palmiers, gougères stuffed with fontina cheese, and soufflé potatoes.

If you're going for Sunday brunch, be prepared for a bit of live music to enliven the meal. Start your brunch with Creole cream cheese Evangeline. This is traditional Creole cream cheese with fruit and granola. There aren't many opportunities to eat Creole cream cheese, and it should be eaten whenever possible. Grillades and grits, waffles, various egg dishes, and a small steak are all part of the brunch menu, and any choice will be a good one.

The desserts that Arnaud's offers are myriad and fit right into the entire experience. The ice creams are lovely, especially the pistachio and the lemon ice. Bananas Foster and café brûlot are prepared tableside. And the strawberries Arnaud are strawberries macerated in port and served over vanilla ice cream, topped with whipped cream. There is clearly no hesitation in gilding the lily.

Arnaud's is an all-around traditional and satisfying experience. When you reach a century in business, there are many traditions and much beauty to preserve.

813 Bienville St.
New Orleans, LA
504-523-5433
arnaudsrestaurant.com

ROCKY & CARLO'S

Oversized portions of classic dishes

St. Bernard Parish is about four miles downriver from the French Quarter. Go just another mile or two and you will be deep in the parish and ready to eat at Rocky & Carlo's. This restaurant is one of the Creole Italian restaurants that New Orleans is known for, celebrating the Sicilian immigration to New Orleans at the turn of the twentieth century. Rocky & Carlo's is known for its oversized portions of classic Creole Italian dishes. Tommy Tommaseo opened this family business with his brother Rocky and his brothers-in-law, Carlo, Mario, and Giuseppe Gioe in 1965.

Before Rocky & Carlo's opened, there was a bar down the street called Angelo's where some of the family worked. Women, however, were not welcome at Angelo's. When Rocky & Carlo's opened they put up a "Ladies Invited" sign that made it clear women were definitely welcome in their restaurant. They sign is still there today. The restaurant still has a reputation for serving all who enter, from regulars to the National Guard. They dedicate themselves to preparing for hurricanes, not only for self-protection, but also to ensure that first responders and others will have a place to eat during the aftermath.

While you're in St. Bernard Parish, visit the Old Arabi Sugar Museum about a block away from the Visitor Center. This little museum tells the story of sugar in St. Bernard Parish and in Louisiana. The museum can be visited during the hours of the Visitor Center; inquire inside for details. The museum is in the shadow of the Domino Sugar Refinery, right on the Mississippi River. This is the largest sugar refinery in North America.

Left: Family and staff.
Right: So much to eat.

The restaurant's most popular dish is macaroni and cheese, which is served with either a brown or red gravy. They produce about twenty-five pounds of macaroni and cheese each day. Keep in mind that an order of macaroni and cheese might feed four people as a side. The rest of the menu includes more Italian dishes like lasagna, meatballs, and eggplant Parmesan. The portions are extraordinarily large. In addition, there are classic New Orleans dishes on the menu, including excellently fried food. The seafood available in St. Bernard Parish is the freshest, since that is where it is caught.

So what might you eat here? Besides the pasta and the Italian favorites and fried Louisiana seafood, there are salads, stuffed peppers, eggplant sticks, and sweet potato sticks. The jambalaya, lasagna, eggplant dressing, and potato salad are all prepared in classic New Orleans ways. And the desserts are as huge as the other portions. A lemon berry mascarpone cake is always a good choice. There are two ice cream cakes: bananas Foster cake and spumoni. Don't miss the caramel cheesecake, either.

Rocky & Carlo's is a meeting place in Chalmette, with a private room where lots of organizations gather for lunch or dinner. No one forgets all that they have done for the community. It is worth a visit.

613 W. St. Bernard Hwy.
Chalmette, LA
504-279-8323

TARTINE NEW ORLEANS

A sandwich shop with more

The term *tartine* comes from the French verb *tartiner,* meaning to spread. Opening a fresh baguette and spreading it with some delicious fresh ingredients—soft cheese, pâté, or even just rich, creamy butter—became synonymous with a sandwich. Now, tartine can mean any kind of open-faced sandwich, and the folks at Tartine New Orleans are making some of the best you can find.

Tartine (the restaurant) is a breakfast and lunch place that is open every day. The husband and wife team owners were educated at the French Culinary Institute in New York. Cara Benson, originally from New Orleans, brought her now husband with her back to her hometown. Cara is the pastry chef, and Evan is the savory chef. Tartine, one of the couple's three restaurants, is an example of a no-frills establishment that serves high-end food. Whether it's the quiche of the day or a bagel or a simple breakfast tartine (brie, jam, and butter), the food is fresh and prepared with the finest ingredients. Today they are very settled into the life of the city with their children, expressing their creativity in their food.

Other tartines on the menu include a pork rillette, which has onion marmalade, a ham tartine with brie and fig mustard, or a salmon rillette with capers, egg, and onion marmalade. All of the tartines are served on baguettes. You can complete your selection with a three-bean salad. Or you can substitute chips, soup, or a small green salad by just adding a dollar to your tab.

Not in the mood for a baguette? Have a sandwich. Perhaps a tuna Niçoise on a brioche. Or a house-smoked turkey sandwich with avocado and Gruyère, with garlic aioli on multigrain bread. A grilled steak sandwich includes pistou (an olive oil–based basil sauce), pickled carrots, and shallots. The salads include the classic tuna Niçoise, embellished with hearts of palm and roasted tomatoes. The shrimp salad has vegetables available during the season with a pistou

Top: Shrimp salad.
Left: French onion soup.

vinaigrette. There is a daily soup. And children may enjoy the very good but kid-friendly peanut butter sandwich, grilled cheese sandwich, or Nutella toast.

Tartine is close to Audubon Park. It's a great place to pick up supplies for a picnic. If you added a bottle of wine and perhaps some fruit, your picnic would be easy and delicious. You can also purchase a whole quiche, charcuterie, and sandwich platters through their catering division.

7217 Perrier St.
New Orleans, LA
504-866-4860
tartineneworleans.com

BAYONA

European and Asian flavors in the French Quarter

This French Quarter restaurant has been serving imaginative New Orleans food for almost thirty years. The flavors that shape the food come from all over Europe with a particular emphasis on the Mediterranean. Susan Spicer, owner and innovator, is constantly layering new flavor over old. The food is all freshly prepared and very particular in its execution. In addition to her commitment to flavor, Chef Spicer is committed to using locally sourced ingredients whenever possible.

Spicer has been cooking professionally since her first job with Daniel Bonnot at Louis XVI Restaurant in 1970. She was peripatetic in her early career, working in California, Paris, and throughout Europe. By 1990 she was ready to open Bayona, which reflects her travels, background, and the sensibilities of New Orleans. All this comes together in Bayona at its French Quarter location with a beautiful courtyard that has been recognized around the world. Spicer is so fundamental to the idea of New Orleans that a character in the New Orleans-based television show, HBO's *Treme,* was modeled after her.

Spicer invented the very best sandwich—duck breast and cashew butter—that ever graced a restaurant menu. Her way with duck, whether grilled or braised, is the stuff of legend. That sandwich remains on the menu by popular demand, even when there was talk of retiring it. The restaurant itself is small, but the courtyard is large and inviting for much of the year. It's tucked into a quiet part of the French Quarter. On Saturdays she serves a really inventive and playful menu, which changes week to week. Not to worry, though, the duck sandwich remains in place.

Two appetizers of note are the eggplant caviar and the sweetbreads. The truffle cheese tart goes in a different direction, but is brimming with flavor. The garlic soup is outstanding—mild and creamy. the shaved pear salad is made to pop with Gruyère cheese. The crab cake salad is very tasty and the boneless pork ribeye is full of flavor. If you

Left: Main dining room in Bayona.

Right: The courtyard at night.

can eat on the courtyard, because the weather permits, you will see lots of light fare on the table. The setting is delightful.

At night the Chinese five spice braised duck is wonderful. The redfish, lamb, sweetbreads, and pork chop are worthy of a try. If you go with a large enough party and spread the choices around, you can share or at least taste all of the choices. Even at fancy New Orleans restaurants, sharing, asking for extra plates, and passing around plates at the table is totally acceptable. When locals eat, they want to share, and the restaurant understands that it means people are enjoying themselves. I have even seen people trade from table to table.

The wine list is very nice and full of unexpected selections. There is an understanding that sparkling wines and rosés are choices that are worthy of selection. In the heat of summer, a crisp, chilled rosé sparkling wine can make the meal very enjoyable and refreshing.

The peanut butter banana pie and the hazelnut torte, as well as the other desserts, are selections that would make you happy, as is the coconut pannacotta called a Japanese cheescake. Even if you are full, the desserts are worth eating. The cheese plate works really well with a dessert wine if you like a savory end to your meal.

This is the place to go for a formal meal that is neither stuffy, nor boring. The service is friendly and efficient, and the wait staff is knowledgeable—how can one resist?

430 Dauphine St.
New Orleans, LA
504-525-4455
bayona.com

LE CROISSANT D'OR PATISSERIE

Excellent French breakfast in the French Quarter

Maurice Delechelle began his baking career at the tender age of fourteen in his hometown of Tours, France, as a pastry apprentice. He traveled around until he landed in New Orleans. In his twenties and weary of life on the road, he decided that a French pastry shop was something that New Orleans needed. In the 1980s he opened Croissant d'Or in the French Quarter, which must have felt like a natural home for the French native. The key to his long-term success may have been his adherence to the rigorous methods he learned back home. "I never try to imitate the local style," he told Nola.com in 2003. "I don't want to change from what I learned."

He prepared French pastries for years until he sold the quaint pâtisserie to his good friend Gerard Marchal, but the transition was seamless because long-time staff was retained. And Chef Delechelle didn't stray too far from the place where he perfected his pâtisserie art—he moved in above Croissant d'Or upon his retirement. Most recently Marchal sold it to Stephanie Doa, and now Chef Sullivan Fournigault lives the pre-dawn life of making classic croissants.

This coffee shop is just what you need in the morning when you get up early and want coffee and a croissant. The croissants are freshly made, sometimes still warm. Served with a steaming cup of coffee, the croissant can be buttered and spread with jam. Or you can choose an almond croissant or a chocolate croissant. There are also various quiches, savory croissants with ham or sausage, and fruit croissants. The Pâtisserie has been there for over thirty years or so, occupying the former home of the Sicilian gelateria, Angelo Brocato's. The Brocato name still greets you from the sidewalk. But once inside you know that

Left: Croquembouche. Credit: Stephen Binns.
Right: Croissant. Credit: Stephen Binns.

you are in a pâtisserie in the French style. On lovely days you can even sit in the small courtyard to enjoy your coffee.

If you are a late riser and arrive in the nebulous time between breakfast and lunch, you might choose the soup of the day. This soup is just as likely to be vegetable soup as a cream of something. Check each day. There is a daily fruit salad as well as a daily green salad. Besides the savory pastries that are available for breakfast, you will find sandwiches on the house-made baguettes or croissants. There could be chicken salad, pâté, sliced chicken, salami and cheese, or tuna salad. These sandwiches are made when ordered. Hot sandwiches can be made with a béchamel on croissant. And then there are the other pastries, all made in the French manner.

Besides the croissant, Croissant d'Or offers fruit tartlets, cookies (don't miss the iced fleur-de-lis cookie), Napoleons, and other traditional French pastries like cream puff financiers. The traditional variations of coffee are on offer, including an iced coffee. There are also hot tea choices, sodas, hot chocolate, fresh lemonade, and bottled juices. And you can always simply buy croissants and baguettes.

617 Ursulines St.
New Orleans, LA
504-524-4663
croissantdornola.com

1000 FIGS

Mediterranean offerings near City Park

Sometimes a food truck becomes so popular that it's time to find a more permanent home for those flavors. That was the case for Gavin Cady and Theresa Galli, whose successful food truck, Fat Falafel, featured all manner of falafel. Now they've taken all of the flavors from those food truck roots and grown them into their own brick and mortar restaurant—the tiny, but wildly popular, 1000 Figs.

It may be small, but those flavors made popular on the food truck scene have only expanded since 1000 Figs opened its doors. The fresh, seasonal dishes are prepared and served as masterfully as works of art. In fact, Cady and Galli have turned the whole restaurant into a veritable local gallery with art adorning the walls, furniture, and even light fixtures all crafted locally. The taste journey, however, will be straight to the eastern Mediterranean, and this trip is guaranteed to satisfy.

The falafel, hummus, and pitas are freshly prepared and the portions are generous. The feast platters are a delectable assortment of stuffed vegetables and fresh slaws, accompanied by olives, pickles, and pita. The usual fare of tzatziki, yogurt, and baba ghanoush can be found. The eggplant in the baba ghanoush has the benefit of being truly smoky and satisfying.

In addition to the eggplant, there are lots of other finely prepared vegetables at 1000 Figs. And for those looking to eat a healthy diet,

1000 Figs is a tiny place, much more popular than its space can accommodate. Conveniently, it's located right next door to Swirl Wines. So if the restaurant is full, place your order, carry a set of silverware, take a seat at one of the tables at Swirl Wines, and order your wine there. The restaurant will deliver your plate to you, and you will have an expansive choice of wines and other drinks to enhance your meal.

Top: Enjoying the food and atmosphere.
Right: A part of the neighborhood.

this is a place to eat well-prepared and beautifully presented food. It's food so good that you forget how healthy it is. And that's the way food should be—good first and healthy second. This restaurant is a rare gem.

1000 Figs is located on the second floor of a small building, which results in a tiny restaurant. 1000 Figs makes the best of its space by lining up the tables against the windows, creating a bright and welcoming space that's always full and bustling. Eating there is a lovely experience, and people linger with pleasure. If you're waiting to pounce on an empty seat, watching diners down another cup of coffee or one last glass of wine can be frustrating. Of course, when it's your turn to sit there, no doubt, you'll be equally as reluctant to leave the table.

3141 Ponce de Leon St.
New Orleans, LA
504-301-0848
1000figs.com

MAYPOP

Where the Mekong meets the Mississippi

The design team at Farouki Farouki knew exactly what they were doing when they created the large map wall at Maypop. From one side, the painting appears to be of the Mekong delta in Southeast Asia. Viewed from the other side, it morphs into the Mississippi Delta. Miles and worlds apart, these two cultures share the river life, and blend here seamlessly in the ingredients and flavors.

Maypop is a light-filled place in the Central Business District that serves New Orleans food with a Vietnamese twist. It is the brainchild of Chef Michael Gulatta. Chef Gulatta is fascinated by the flavors of Vietnam and New Orleans. He's exploring a palate that is very New Orleans based, but with a modern and outward-looking attitude.

At lunch you can find such fusions of flavor as crab gumbo served with sticky rice and fermented black beans, wok-fried egg noodle with jumbo shrimp, or braised lamb with coconut milk. The flavors and presentation are recognizable to a New Orleanian, but have the additional aspect that reflects the changes in the food of New Orleans brought on by the influx of immigrants from Vietnam in the 1970s. Though to be clear, this is not a Vietnamese restaurant, but rather a new creation born of the influences that the two cultures have on one another in New Orleans.

The use of fermented beans, lemon grass, noodle bowls, pickled vegetables, cumin, and saffron with local ingredients adds a respectful nod to Asia. The menu contains dim sum, inventive cocktails, and dessert made with miso. A trip to Maypop is a special dining experience in a modernist setting. The restaurant is light and airy with a very strong modern sensibility. The plates, napery, and the utensils all present as modern, yet they are still comfortable and not awkward, as some modernist tableware can be.

For lunch, the fusion is apparent in the pork belly macaroni and cheese made with coconut milk béchamel. The sheepshead with

Pasta Maypop.

crawfish is also served with fermented black beans. The crab gumbo is served with sticky rice. Any of these things would make for a delightful lunch that merges flavors from two deltas.

At dinner, hand-pulled noodles served with crab and pork is finished with Maypop sauce. Cured lemon fish is served with pickled mirliton. A salad of Bibb lettuce is dressed with coconut cucumber ranch dressing. The innovative mixing of flavors is obviously intentional, but subtle and delicious. It's hard not to fall in love with this food.

The wine list is deep enough for any wine maven. The house cocktails are also interesting. The bar carries sparkling wines and beers. And for dessert, there is a dark chocolate cake with blood orange. The Maypop pie has a gingersnap crust and a five-spice meringue.

Maypop has a dim sum brunch each Saturday and Sunday. Head cheese and crab soup dumplings, octopus and turnip cakes, calamari with tamarind sauce, lamb dumplings, and crabmeat toast with fried eggs are just a few of the offerings. It all makes eating a delight.

611 O'Keefe Ave.
New Orleans, LA
504-518-6345
maypoprestaurant.com

PORT OF CALL

Hands down the best hamburger in the city

Port of Call restaurant and bar is visited by hipsters, tourists, and older French Quarter residents alike. It's easy to forget that the restaurant is in an historic building and that the restaurant itself is over fifty years old, having opened in 1963. The restaurant is so sure of itself, so very much defined, that it seems timeless, not historic. It was owned early on by George Brumat, who fed many of the French Quarter workers after their shifts let out later in the evenings. They would come for a steak or a burger, which was ground on site using the steak scraps that accumulated when the steaks were trimmed. Brumat was not making a statement about grinding your own burgers for a better product—he was simply frugal. Just by being good and continuing to serve its clients, it has become a landmark.

What is it? It's a steakhouse and burger joint. It has been recognized as Zagat Survey's Best Burger. Gambit and CitySearch have also named the Port of Call burger as the Best Burger in New Orleans. They embrace the idea of being a burger joint with their casual dress and service—not inattentive, just casual. It's a wonderful place to take children, who can play outside on the sidewalk as you might wait awhile for a table. Port of Call does not take reservations.

This simple, straightforward place serves three different steaks. There's New York strip steak, ribeye, and filet mignon. You select the degree to which it is cooked and how your potato is served. There are two burgers with variation—the hamburger, mushroom burger, and either one of those with cheese. Those mushrooms are sautéed in wine sauce, making them the fanciest item on the whole menu. These hamburgers are monsters of eight ounces of freshly ground meat. You can be sure that the meat is excellent, and you can be confident in the degree to which it is cooked.

The bar serves mostly punch-like drinks that it has perfected and that regulars have come to expect. The tiki influence is very strong and

14

Top left: A filet and loaded potato
Bottom left: Mushroom burger.
Right: A New Orleans cocktail.

the house drinks tend to the sweet. The bar can make you a traditional drink, so have no fear. However, this is not a new craft cocktail bar. The beers are limited and not craft beers.

Your salad will have any of the standard choices of restaurant dressings. The baked potato can be piled high with every sort of topping: sour cream, cheese, mushrooms, chives, or bacon bits. They don't nickel and dime you for your choices; there's no charge. But there's no side of French fries—the fryer broke a long time ago, and it hasn't been replaced.

838 Esplanade Ave.
New Orleans, LA
504-523-0120
portofcallnola.com

TURKEY AND THE WOLF

Modern flavors in the big city

You'd be hard pressed to find any trace of pretension at Turkey and the Wolf. From the comic mural outside the Irish Channel restaurant, to the simple menu classifications of "Sandwiches" or "Not Sandwiches," and even the mismatched kitschy cutlery, this place is all about having a good time. Perhaps ironically, it's also received its fair share of highbrow recognition since its 2017 opening—even named Best New Restaurant that year by *Food & Wine* magazine. While some have called it "gas station food," you'll want to do more than just drive by this colorful sandwich shop.

Mason Hereford has taken his culinary experience at high-end restaurants combined with his inspiration eating at small-town Virginia roadside delis and applied it to create a sandwich shop that has a slick restaurant sensibility. It's playful about what it is with eyes wide open about the irony of making casual food with a fancy twist. And it's dead serious about looking for flavor and interesting combinations. The place is decorated in a style that's eclectic and fun. Nothing matches, but somehow it all fits together. Clearly Hereford had a desire to thumb his nose at convention, and he accomplishes this without leaving out flavor.

The self-deprecation is reflected in dishes like tacos inauthenticos, designed to share with the table. It includes hog's head cheese and really good tortillas. Is it authentic—no. But who cares? The hand pie, which is listed as fried pot pie, is also really good. The very veggie sandwich is called a collard green melt. It's thickly layered with smothered collards, coleslaw, and Swiss cheese on toasted rye.

On the "Not Sandwiches" list, there are deviled eggs topped with fried chicken skin—a great side for any sandwich. There's a wedge salad with bacon and chunky blue cheese dressing and a few more choices. Dessert is vanilla soft serve with a variety of toppings like tahini and date molasses or even savory snack foods.

Left: Sandwich.
Right: Deviled eggs and a beer.

The menu is small. The presentation—and in fact the whole place—is simple, but the prices are very reasonable and there's a feeling of fun there. Chefs from other local restaurants tend to hang out there, because there's nothing fancy or superfluous about it. Have a cocktail from the ever-changing cocktail menu. Embrace that, and your mouth will really be happy. This is a real sandwich shop without table service. But the food is so good, you'll be happy as soon as it hits your lips. It seems crazy to recognize a sandwich shop as one of the Best New Restaurants, but that just tells you something about how good it must be.

739 Jackson Ave.
New Orleans, LA
504-218-7428
turkeyandthewolf.com

COCHON

A modern Cajun bastion in New Orleans

This award-winning Cajun restaurant, part of the Link Restaurant Group, was opened shortly after Hurricane Katrina. When the city re-opened, Donald Link found himself with a restaurant in mid-renovation with no immediate prospects for local or tourist customers. To his credit, he moved forward with his renovation and opened in the crippled city. Cochon has been operating, and even thriving, since them. It is very Cajun forward, thus it makes a good place to learn about the basic flavors of Cajun food. The menu includes alligator, oysters, and fried livers with pepper jelly. The food is heavily seasoned, but not overtly spicy.

Donald Link has created a place within the city that really interprets Cajun food for New Orleanians. It's a bit too fancy for a Cajun restaurant in Cajun country, but it hits just the right note for an urban setting. Link's family is rooted in the land and in the Cajun food traditions. Donald started washing dishes in restaurants when he was fifteen years old. He moved to San Francisco to continue his culinary training in restaurants and at the California Culinary Academy. He worked at a number of places, but he did some work bringing the food of Louisiana to California. The return to New Orleans was the natural next step, and with his training and family connections, Cochon has the very best boudin and other traditional family dishes to share with its visitors.

The food includes ribs, family-made boudin, pork cheeks, grits, and shrimp. Ham, pig, and fish are all presented in one form or another.

> Be sure to ask your server about the special pairings of cocktails, wine, and beer with your meal. Cochon has made a real effort to ensure that your alcohol choices can match well with your food.

Left: Dining room.
Right: Ham hock.

And there is the famous oyster and bacon sandwich. It is a masterpiece. It's so good that it's sometimes hard to select anything else on return visits. Sides include lima beans, greens, shrimp with eggplant dressing, and macaroni and cheese.

The restaurant is full of people enjoying their food. The drinks are generous. The beer and wine lists are extensive, especially stocked with drinks that will match the intense flavors in the food. The wait staff is knowledgeable and busy. They can help you navigate the restaurant, the wine list, the cocktails, and the beer selections. Sometimes people worry about pairing boudin balls or fried oysters with wine, but this is a place with a wine list that will help dispel any worries about such pairings.

Desserts at Cochon are not to be missed. They also reflect the Cajun roots of the place. Strawberry shortcake, for example, is served with mascarpone. Chocolate beignets served with sweet Vietnamese coffee is another very local treat. Malted milk cake and pineapple upside-down cake are also on offer.

Cochon, open at lunch and dinner, is located in the warehouse district. It is an award-winning restaurant that celebrates Cajun food values in the city.

930 Tchoupitoulas St.
New Orleans, LA
504-588-7675
cochonrestaurant.com

BRENNAN'S

Breakfast at Brennan's is a real treat

Owen Brennan, the eldest sibling in the Brennan family dynasty, conceived the idea for Brennan's Restaurant. He worked with all of his siblings at the Old Absinthe House, a bar that you can still find in the French Quarter. There he was teased by the owner of another restaurant, Arnaud's, that he was "too Irish" to be able to run a fine restaurant and should stick with a bar. Owen stepped right up to the challenge and opened a fine-dining restaurant. First, he opened Brennan's Vieux Carré Restaurant, and he and his family set about creating what was to become Brennan's. After his untimely death, his wife and children took over the restaurant in 1946 while Owen's siblings moved to Commander's Palace and other restaurants. Brennan's came to be known for its breakfast, with the phrase "Breakfast at Brennan's" vying with novelist Frances Parkinson Keyes's *Dinner at Antoine's*.

Breakfast at Brennan's became a great success. There are eggs—eggs Sardou, eggs Cardinal, eggs Owen—and fish, chicken, and French toast, to name a few of the huge selection of choices. Breakfast has some tasty cocktail eye openers—not just traditional morning drinks like Bloody Marys. Brennan's brings milk punch, many coffee choices,

Bananas Foster is a classic dessert at Brennan's, traditionally set ablaze tableside in a dimmed dining room. The dish is said to have been invented by Ella Brennan when the family was at Brennan's Vieux Carré Restaurant, preparing to open Brennan's. It's named for Richard Foster, owner of the Foster Awning Company, a friend of Owen's and frequent diner at Brennan's. These spiced, rum-flambéed bananas served over ice cream have become a New Orleans classic. Watching a table next to you have this dish prepared can prompt your table to say, "I'll have what they are having."

Left: Exterior.
Center: Eggs Hussarde. Credit: RBRG.
Right: Bananas Foster. Credit: Ralph Brennan Restaurant.

and house-made sodas to the table. If you are not ready to eat a large meal at breakfast, just think of it as brunch. It does not call breakfast, "brunch." Brennan's opens at 8 a.m. on the weekends, so there is truth in the phrase, "Breakfast at Brennan's."

If you pop into Brennan's for lunch or dinner, there are still many inspired choices beyond eggs. Gumbo, lobster, steak, lamb, duck, and chicken are all available for your plate. And for dessert there is the famous bananas Foster, crepes, bread pudding, and other choices like seasonal sorbet. Chef Slade Rushing, the executive chef, has maintained the famous dishes, but he has updated the menu for modern palates. The French Quarter restaurant has many rooms for private dining and a lovely courtyard—popular for wedding celebrations. Upstairs rooms overlook the courtyard, so the view can be enjoyed throughout.

The bar, under the watchful eye of Lu Brow, is exceptional. It's a nice spot for a drink and a tasty something like a cheese plate to nibble on. The drinks reach into the past, but they are light reinventions of the classics. The Roost Bar opens at 9 a.m. on weekdays so breakfast diners are able to order an eye-opener.

417 Royal St.
New Orleans, LA
504-525-9711
brennansneworleans.com

ST. JAMES CHEESE COMPANY

Cheese, cheese, cheese!

Sometimes you don't want to eat a big meal, but you shouldn't have to sacrifice flavor. Whether eating a light lunch or a light dinner, St. James Cheese Company makes a small meal as important as a big one. There are two locations of St. James Cheese, so it is possible to enjoy the place, no matter where you are in the city. In the land of St. James, cheese is king.

The king's loyal subjects are none other than owners Richard and Danielle Sutton, who know cheese inside and out. The adventure began for them in a two-hundred-year-old cheese shop in London's St. James neighborhood. Gradually they've built a veritable empire of cheese spanning two continents by focusing on relationships with cheese mongers far and wide who felt as passionately about the product as they did. Luckily for New Orleanians, they've opened special stores where you can buy cheese that is ripe and ready to eat today or for a party in a week.

Cheese is the center of the St. James universe, but there is so much more. The uptown location has delightful sandwiches like roast beef and house-smoked blue cheese. The Colby on sourdough can be amended with ham, bacon, or prosciutto. Salads all include cheese, naturally. And the cheese boards are imaginative and served at just the right temperature and at the right time, depending on the cheese. Can you imagine eating in a cheese shop and not having house-made macaroni and cheese, prepared with their own blend of cheeses? Everything is served with craft beers, cider, or wine. This is a place where you can eat in or take out for a picnic. There are so many parks in the city, and this makes a delightful way to sit under spreading oak trees or by lagoons to enjoy a meal.

Left: Eating at St. James.
Right: Owners Richard and Danielle Sutton.

The warehouse district store downtown serves brunch on Sunday. Pickled shrimp as well as roasted vegetables are not cheese-centric, so if you visit with a person who is not ready for cheese, you can find lovely choices. However, for those who want it, there is the Monte Cristo with its cheese and powdered sugar, lemon ricotta pancakes, or pan-fried pâté. Try the Red Eye, whether your eyes are red or not, with its grits, egg, corn maque choux, and blistered tomatoes. What a tasty brunch to help you start off your day.

Eat cheese as a snack or a meal. The cheese here is excellent. The variety is amazing. You will not be disappointed.

5004 Prytania St. (Uptown)
641 Tchoupitoulis St. (Downtown)
New Orleans, LA
504-899-4737
stjamescheese.com

TOUPS SOUTH

Dinner and exhibits

This Pan-Southern restaurant with a Cajun attitude is located inside of the Southern Food & Beverage Museum. The chef is Isaac Toups, who, with his wife, Amanda, opened the restaurant in 2016. It was his second foray into the restaurant business after the success of Toups' Meatery. This James Beard Foundation finalist and former finalist and fan favorite on *Top Chef* (season 2016), Chef Toups has created a menu that is both creative and comforting. Drawing deeply on his Cajun roots, Chef Toups offers some must-haves on his menu, in particular his sourdough biscuits with crab fat butter and his cracklins. Dishes for the table are a regular part of eating here. His stack of pork chops is fit for the entire table.

Toups South is integrated into the Southern Food & Beverage Museum insofar as it is educational and fun to eat there, as well as rewarding by way of taste. The kitchen is open and surrounded by a counter. Sitting at the counter allows diners to enjoy the theater of the kitchen, actually ask questions of the chef and staff, and feel satisfied that all the dishes are authentic and real. This makes sitting at the counter almost an exhibit within the museum. In addition, the bar is

The Southern Food & Beverage Museum is a unique museum dedicated to the celebration of the food of the American South. Each state is represented in this old market building, with a particular emphasis on the food and drink of New Orleans and Louisiana. After all, that is where you are. The collection of the Museum of the American Cocktail and the Galerie de l'Absinthe both offer smart and interesting history with lots of artifacts. And the kitchen allows the visitor to take lunchtime classes on Mondays and Thursdays. www.natfab.org.

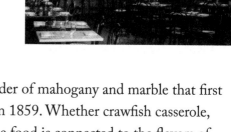

Top: Crab salad. Credit: Denny Culbert.
Right: Getting ready for service. Credit:
Denny Culbert.

the mid-nineteenth century wonder of mahogany and marble that first graced the restaurant Bruning's in 1859. Whether crawfish casserole, crab salad, steak frites, or goat, the food is connected to the flavors of the South.

The cocktail menu is full of whimsy, with a Toups julep and porkchops and applesauce, which is a pork-washed whiskey with apple. But if you have a hankering for traditional cocktails, they can be produced. And the wine list, personally selected by Amanda Toups, provides wines that pair well with the hamburger and the house-made pastrami. It is all-around satisfying.

1504 Oretha Castle Haley Blvd.
New Orleans, LA
504-304-2147
toupssouth.com

ANDREA'S

Eat all over Italy right in New Orleans

When the classics are truly mastered, the quality of the dishes speaks volumes. It's why Andrea Apuzzo brings the time-honored traditions of European chefs to his eponymous restaurant. This means that since its founding in 1985, he has been a constant presence in the kitchen: overseeing the preparation and even serving the Italian food that's made his restaurant famous. His presence is felt in every fiber of the establishment.

Chef Andrea learned these techniques from his birthplace, on the Isle of Capri. After working at restaurants around Europe, he came to America to work at hotels in Atlanta and in New Orleans. Finally, he opened his own restaurant, Andrea's, in 1985. His books, *La Cucina di Andrea's* and *Andrea's Light Cookbook*, are local favorites, while the restaurant itself has been recognized with the *Wine Spectator* Award of Excellence and the Distinguished Restaurants of North America (DiRona) Award of Excellence.

Any local will notice that there are also Creole dishes on the menu, evidence that Chef Andrea knows his clientele and recognizes a delicious dish when he encounters one. When these Creole dishes are served, however, it is in the Creole manner. The Italian dishes, in turn, remain starkly in their own style, typically Northern Italian. Chef Andrea allows each dish to shine in its own right, no fusion required.

In keeping with the chef's tireless work ethic, the restaurant is open daily for lunch or brunch and dinner. Contrast the gumbo and turtle soup, both squarely Creole, with the minestrone Milanese and zuppa di cannellini, both very Italian. They can both exist on the menu, but they're not merged in order to best honor tradition and highlight the freshly made ingredients.

The long lunch menu harkens back to the tradition of a large meal at midday. It includes heavier fare such as veal scallopine Romano

Left: Softshell crab.
Right: Osso buco.

and eggplant Parmesan, along with lighter options like crabmeat and artichoke salad or baked chicken. And naturally, pizza is an option!

Dinner boasts an even wider selection of seafood, veal, beef, lamb, and mussels. The old style osso bucco is a classic choice. Each dish can be complemented with sides such as spinach, cauliflower, asparagus, and angel-hair pasta. Don't forget the equally well curated children's menu, for the little bambini with big appetites.

If you haven't filled up yet, you'll want to leave room to sample the extensive dessert menu. It includes the expected gelato, tiramisu, cassata, zuppa Inglese, and the New Orleans favorite—bread pudding. The wine list rivals the dessert menu in its depth and breadth. Many of the wines are Italian and very well selected to pair with the menu as a whole.

Andrea's is a very popular restaurant with a loyal local following that keeps Chef Andrea coming in day after day. Together they've made this Old World treasure into a timeless classic.

3100 19th St.
Metairie, LA
504-834-8583
andreasrestaurant.com

CURE

The home of the new cocktail in New Orleans

Sometimes you want to go cocktail forward and have food that supports your beverage of choice. When that mood hits you, go straight to Cure, the drinks emporium that mixes great traditional cocktails and delicious innovations. With that attention to flavor in your glass, you can expect delicious food on your plate. Cure is only open in the evenings and for happy hour Friday through Sunday.

Cure cofounder Neal Bodenheimer left New Orleans when he turned eighteen to explore the world. He traveled to the places on his must-see list, ultimately returning stateside to work in Manhattan at the Atlantic Grill as a mixologist. Like many who saw their city in need, he returned home to New Orleans to help rebuild the city after Hurricane Katrina in 2006, finding a reason to put down roots again. The choice of Freret Street on which to build his own cocktail restaurant was prescient, becoming one of the neighborhood anchors amidst its rapid growth. Together with his cofounders Kirk Estopinal, and Matthew Kohnke, they've built a new kind of cocktail restaurant that harkens back to the old, medicinal days of cocktail invention— hence its healing name. Substance and style meet a curiosity for old traditions and a meticulous approach to healthful and interesting food pairing. For its efforts, Cure has been recognized by the James Beard Foundation, winning the Best Bar Program award in 2018.

Whether you eat bar snacks like deviled eggs "cacao e pepe" or the midnight Cuban, you will not be disappointed. The cheese plates

Cure is known in New Orleans as the first place that was devoted solely to the new and modern cocktail. Today the owner, Neal Bodenheimer, is deeply involved in Tales of the Cocktail, a popular annual trade conference in New Orleans for the cocktail and spirit industry.

Left: Beet and radish jewels.
Right: A mint julep. Credit: Sharon Pye.

and charcuterie are outstanding. The smoke trout dip allows you to nibble, or you can choose Nonna's meatballs when you want to eat a bit heartier fare. The chicken liver pâté with fig mostarda is also a bit hearty. The sardines are a special treat. And the famous chocolate truffle, paired with a sweet drink, is a wonderful and sophisticated end to the evening. No matter what you decide to drink, you will find something delicious to pair with it.

The house drinks have a wide range, including house standards, but the bar chefs add specials and change the menu as the seasons change and local ingredients reach their peak freshness. If you are a one-drink drinker, the bar chefs will help you. They have a depth of knowledge of classic cocktails and will do whatever it takes to make you happy.

They also have low-proof cocktails and non-alcoholic beer, which allows you to pace yourself. There is an interesting beer list, for those who want a beer and a shot. You can pair your beer and spirits.

4905 Freret St.
New Orleans, LA
504-302-2357
curenola.com

SALON BY SUCRÉ

A mid-century modern eating spot in the French Quarter

The folks behind Sucré, Joel Dondis and Tariq Hanna, have a way with design as well as flavor. Salon, located upstairs from the patisserie Sucré on Conti Street in the French Quarter, transports diners to mid-century Paris. It is a truly beautiful spot decorated in French mid-century modern style, which is the note that they wanted to play. The gleaming marble bar and the crisp white tablecloths become the blank canvas on which your meal will be the true work of art. Sitting inside the dining space feels like Paris. So many places in New Orleans claim to have Parisian connections, but this place feels as if you've landed in a little café in the very posh Saint-Germain.

While its sister patisserie Sucré downstairs will send you on your way with sweets, Salon plays to its savory strengths and has become particularly successful with the bustling brunch crowd. Former executive Chef Hanna said it best, "If you become insanely busy for brunch, why not be a brunch restaurant? It makes sense." Once you've sampled their croque Benedict with raclette on a chive biscuit, it'll make sense to you too.

Salon is THE spot for mid-afternoon tea. You can have sandwiches, baked goods, and sweet bits served with tea, a cocktail, or sparkling wine. The menu is seasonal, so it is constantly being reinvented, but expect sliders, sandwiches, and quiches on the savory menu. It's likely that the menu will include flavored madeleines. And the chocolates, macarons, and patisserie all complete the tea. All of the food is presented as beautifully as the surroundings. And the flavor is precise and delicious. The menu isn't large, but it contains a wonderful balance of savory and sweet offerings that reflects the attention to detail, like its surroundings.

Left: Prosciutto frittata. Credit: Sam Hanna.
Right: The inviting entrance. Credit: Sam Hanna.

Besides tea, there is a brunch menu that is more traditionally substantial. You can expect waffles and chicken; an oyster, bacon, lettuce, and tomato sandwich; and, of course, that famous croque Benedict. You can order a charcuterie plate or granola. Cheesecake, white chocolate bread pudding, and other wonderful desserts are enticements. And why eat at Salon if don't intend to eat dessert? If you're a dessert lover, this is the place to come. Brunch is accompanied by mimosas, and this can extend your stay at Salon, perhaps indefinitely.

Unexpectedly, this café has extensive cocktails—including tea-based cocktails—and an excellent wine list. Both the cocktails and the special wine list are very much selected to complement the desserts. The wine list contains wines by the glass, which enhance the enjoyment of the sweets on offer.

622 B Conti St. (Upstairs)
New Orleans, LA
504-267-7098
restaurantsucre.com

GW FINS

The fishmonger czar of the South

A changing menu dictated by nature itself, prepared by chefs with a renowned intolerance for anything but the absolute freshest ingredients sets GW Fins on a plane above all other restaurants of the same ilk. In fact, Chef Tenney Flynn is so meticulous about the fish he serves that he was called the "fishmonger czar of the South" by the *Wall Street Journal*. And it's a well-deserved moniker. Even local fish sellers go first to GW Fins with their seafood, because they know if their fish isn't fresh, it will not be accepted.

Consistently voted the best seafood restaurant in New Orleans, GW Fins is not a restaurant tethered to the New Orleans canon of dishes. This place is all about fresh seafood. It's about in-house butchering of the freshest seafood and the maximum use of the fish from one end to the other. This is not a nod to frugality, but rather an acknowledgment that just eating fish fillets is lazy eating. Some of the best parts of the fish are also the most overlooked. And the use of the whole fresh fish offers the most intense flavors.

GW Fins is an elegant, understated restaurant without distractions taking attention away from conversation and the art on the table. That isn't to say it's boring. The decor is an enhancement of the dining experience. The menu changes depending on the freshest ingredients available. It's certainly heavy with Gulf of Mexico seafood, but not limited to local fish. This is the place to visit when you want an elegant meal, you don't need a New Orleans food fix, and you love and appreciate fish prepared as the star of the plate.

It's difficult to be specific about the menu at the restaurant, because the menu changes depending on the availability and the freshness of the fish that is delivered daily. Of course, knowing that the fish will be the freshest—even without knowing what specific fish will be available—makes a trip to GW Fins more exciting. It's part adventure and all pleasure.

Wood-grilled pompano with melon salsa, blue crab fritters, and chili oil.

As the perfect accompaniment to the seafood entrees, the wine list at GW Fins is also outstanding, having been recognized by *Wine Spectator* many times. The wines come from around the world, so you're likely to find something new on the list. There are many wines available by the glass.

Appetizers come cold and hot. The hot types include, when available, seafood gumbo, fried shrimp with green apple slaw, barbecue shrimp and grits, and soft shell crab. If you prefer your seafood raw or cold, try tuna tartare, tataki, ceviche, and tuna tacos. There are always specials. Salads include a shrimp remoulade or an heirloom tomato salad. Scalibut, a unique marriage of halibut and sea scallop, is something divine and unexpected. If it's available, you should get it. Snapper, tuna, drum, swordfish, and salmon were all found on a recent menu. Meat is available, for those so inclined. If you want a steak, pork chop, or even chicken, you will find it well prepared and ready to stand up to the fish dishes. There are also a number of notable side dishes, like the mashed sweet potatoes, fixed with bourbon, banana, and vanilla, and a wonderful mushroom risotto. For dessert do not leave without the salty malty ice cream pie. It's decadent enough to make your "last-meal list."

808 Bienville St.
New Orleans, LA
504-581-3467
gwfins.com

DRAGO'S SEAFOOD RESTAURANT

The charbroiled oyster capital

The best family businesses are the ones where the loyal customers know the whole family by name, and vice versa. That's been the case at Drago's for more than forty years, and it doesn't show any signs of stopping now that the second generation of the family is taking the reins. Croatian founders Drago and Klara Cvitanovich knew they loved serving up the best oysters, though they had no idea how popular their little suburban restaurant would someday become.

The restaurant was originally in Metairie, in the suburbs, but now also has a branch in the Hilton Riverside. The original location is full of locals getting their fill of food prepared with a lot of care and served by a staff who feel like part of the family. In 1969 the Cvitanoviches opened Drago's Seafood Restaurant, which people returned to repeatedly because of its great value and great food. Although Drago is no longer with us, his son, Tommy, is on the scene, keeping the flame of tradition alive.

The family has roots in the oyster business, so they know a thing or two about them. It's no wonder that the restaurant is oyster-forward, famous for the original charbroiled oyster—gently broiled with a delicious sauce, served hot and cooked, but still tender and juicy with that lovely sauce. Their raw oysters are impeccably fresh and briny from the sea. Oysters Voisin is the marriage of all things delicious—fried oysters, creamed spinach, bacon bordelaise sauce, and cheese.

The appetizers present almost everything that the water has to offer. That includes fried alligator to fried squid, with shrimp, tuna, and crab dip in-between onion rings and spinach dip. The menu is really extensive, so there is no point in thinking that the choices won't have something for everyone. There's a whole fried seafood menu, which offers traditional platters. There are gumbos, soups, and salads for those

Charbroiled oysters grilling.
Credit: Brett Bauman.

who want something a bit lighter. The mixed grill—a filet, lobster, and shrimp—is one of the go-to dishes after charbroiled oysters. Shrimp stuffed with boudin blurs the line between Creole and Cajun. And the duck breast and oysters over pasta is made in heaven.

You can find traditional shrimp creole, crawfish étouffée, and grillades and grits made with veal. The corn maque choux, the red beans and rice, and charbroiled corn on the cob are just sides, but feel like main plates. In other words, you are in good hands.

The restaurant in the Hilton is much bigger than the Metairie location, and it caters to people downtown, but you're more likely to find the Cvitanovich family at the Metairie location.

Lunch includes lots of po'boys, gumbo, and the usual plates we consider a New Orleans lunch. And desserts are just as special—and traditional—as the rest of the fare. The hot brownie à la mode is meant to be shared. The crème brûlée is just like your grandmother would remember it. The cheesecake is memorable, as is the praline parfait. They have adequate beer and wine lists. And the whole staff loves to see children enjoying the bounty of New Orleans food, so bring a child or grandchild with you.

3232 N. Arnoult Rd.
Metairie, LA
504-888-9254

Hilton New Orleans Riverside
2 Poydras St.
504-584-3911

dragosrestaurant.com

CAFÉ AT THE SQUARE

An oasis in the CBD

Imagine finding the perfect place of respite in the Central Business District. A bright place from which you can look out on the world around you. A place to pop in out of the weather at happy hour,. A cozy space to just relax over a meal. This is what David Smith and Doug Hary imagined for the Café at the Square—casual comfort food, right in the middle of the bustling CBD.

Finding such a classic American place downtown is a welcome surprise. This is the place to find a great, never-frozen burger or another excellent sandwich, good soups, and other café delights. Café at the Square is a good place for breakfast. The waffles with strawberries and cream are a good way to start the day. Granola, real oatmeal, and French toast are all available, as well as an assortment of egg variations from scrambled eggs to omelets. Eating a BLT—bacon, lettuce, and tomato—sandwich for breakfast with a side of grits is a way to eat lunch and breakfast at the same time.

The Café has been recently renovated, and it's bright, shiny, and inviting. For lunch, you might try the French onion soup. This is intensely flavored and cheesy. The fried green tomatoes with shrimp could be a meal in and of itself, forget that it's on the starter menu. The crab cake salad offers you two crab cakes over a salad of greens with cucumbers and tomatoes. For those on a perennial diet, there is a resolution salad—simple greens and a protein of your choice.

You can order a green tomato BLT—bacon, lettuce, and fried green tomatoes on bread. The slightly sour taste of the green tomatoes add an interesting twist to the BLT. Another interesting twist on the BLT is the BLTA, which adds avocado to the traditional sandwich. And there's a crab cake version that gilds the lily with crab cakes on the BLT base.

Top left: Asian tuna salad with wasabi vinaigrette.

Bottom left: Hamburger steak with onions, mushrooms, and gravy.

Right: Chicken Lafayette.

The entrées are interesting, too, with the Grecian chicken being a particularly delightful choice. If you are interested in the specials, check the website, which is kept up to date. And if you're there during happy hour, there's special pricing on the house wine, discounted appetizers, and beers, well drinks, and rum punch for very reduced prices. Give it a try.

500 St. Charles Ave.
New Orleans, LA
504-304-7831
cafeatthesquare.com

STEIN'S MARKET & DELI

As close to New York as you can get in New Orleans

Walking into Stein's really does remind me of a proper New York deli. It doesn't really look like one—it looks like a market and deli, as its name implies. But it smells just like a New York deli. And that smell brings your mind right to the Big Apple. It's open early and closes for an early dinner, but not so early that you can't make it there after work to pick up some delicious meat. Dan Stein gave up the practice of law to open and run a shop that brings new and authentic elements to New Orleans. He opened not long after the city was getting back on its feet after Hurricane Katrina and has offered a special place for great food and beer to the city.

Breakfast is all about the bagel. Not just any bagels, these Davidovich bagels come straight from New York City. Treat yourself to one with smoked salmon, flavored cream cheese, or even butter and jam. You can get one or more of the many types of bagel: whole wheat, sesame seed, the everything, onion, cinnamon, and even gluten-free. The cream cheese choices are myriad: sun-dried tomato, roasted garlic and onion, smoked salmon, honey nut, and jalapeño cheddar to name a few.

Sandwiches include an Italian hoagie, which will give the traditional muffuletta a run for its money. Stein's own "muphuletta" is made with house-made olive salad and it should not be ashamed. Corned beef, pastrami, bacon, ham, prosciutto, turkey, roast beef, tongue, a veggie sandwich, tuna melt, egg salad, and a Caprese all make ordering lunch a head-scratching moment. Luckily, everyone is in the same boat, trying to decide between the usual order and something new that seems compelling.

The salads, all of which could be an entire lunch, border on the enormous. They are made fresh and combine some innovative ingredients. The spring salad contains an orange vinaigrette, pickled

Left: Making sandwiches.

Right: Beer and wine in the market.

fennel, and goat cheese. The xim salad contains kale and Brussels sprouts. The side salads are very deli. They include potato salad, pasta salad, cole slaw, chicken salad, tuna salad, and egg salad. You can get sauerkraut by the pound. Chopped liver, pickled tomato, and a knish are just waiting to be ordered.

The matzo ball soup has a place next to gazpacho. It is really a deli, but there are enough non-deli items to make a person understand that it is not New York. And every day there is a sandwich special. If you're taking things home, you can also pick up some mustard or pickles to add to your meal and keep in your larder.

The beer selection is really outstanding. There is local beer, and also barrel-aged stout and saisons. Most beer can be bought by the bottle, so you can take it home for your own refrigerator. There are also beer-making classes. They are very interested in beer, so if you want something that isn't carried at the deli, they are open to investigating it.

And then there is Whatever Coffee. This is the shop within the shop that makes Stein's a real treasure. It isn't open all day, but it serves very carefully curated coffee. It is purchased in small batches to make sure that it is fresh. So, for good sandwiches, good coffee, and good beer: Stein's.

2207 Magazine St.
New Orleans, LA
504-527-0771
steinsdeli.com

BLUE OAK BARBECUE

Good, no *excellent*, barbecue in New Orleans

New Orleans is not famous for its barbecue. It's not really a barbecue town. It is rich in tradition, but not that tradition. So Blue Oak Barbecue is a surprise. But no matter how much you may love Creole food or even Cajun food, sometimes you need to have something different. When the need for smoked meat that is well seasoned hits you, there's no need for a major road trip. All you need to do is make your way to Blue Oak Barbecue.

Blue Oak was opened in its present location by Philip Mosely and Ronnie Evans after they had tested their mettle with a regular pop-up at the music club, Chickie Wah Wah. Before that, the thoroughly New Orleans boys invested the time to learn about barbecue in Vail, Colorado. Based on their low-and-slow skills, and even though the music at the club was popular, the temptation of oaky barbecue and a famous ginger sesame slaw and a jerk pork sandwich drew its own fans. The barbecue customers followed the pair to North Carrollton Avenue, where you can still get the slaw and the jerk sandwich. They've expanded their offerings as they've gotten comfortable in their own digs.

There are lots of choices and variations on barbecue here. Try the smoked wings or the nachos, which change daily. This is a beef barbecue place, so you can rely on the brisket, either chopped or sliced. There is chicken and also ribs, fixed St. Louis style. There is also pulled pork, which you will find on a sandwich or on your meat plate. Your food comes on a traditional metal tray with sliced white bread, pickles, crackers, onions, and sides. So what are the sides? There is, of course, coleslaw made with ginger and sesame, barbecue beans, macaroni and cheese that is enhanced with roasted garlic, and potato salad. And there are roasted Brussels sprouts. Philip and Ronnie have taken side dishes to a new level as compared with other barbecue joints.

The burger is made with ground brisket, so it's full of flavor. Add to that meat, caramelized onions and cheese, and you have a really

Top: All things barbecue.
Right: The owners.

wonderful burger. There's a chicken sandwich made with pulled chicken with slaw, onions, and pickles. A sausage sandwich is available, but you can take it to another level by adding pulled pork or chopped brisket. This place is a meat palace. Don't forget about the smoked chicken salad, which is elevated by the smoked flavor. It is a delightful and flavorful surprise.

There is beer, shots, and house wine. This isn't the place to do your fancy drinking, but the margaritas and daiquiris go really well with that smoky-flavored meat.

900 N. Carrollton Ave.
New Orleans, LA
504-822-2583
blueoakbbq.com

DTB

Down the Bayou on Oak Street

DTB is short for Down the Bayou. And that is what a trip to DTB is, right in the middle of the city. The restaurant calls its food Coastal Cajun Cuisine. The owners, Jacob Naquin and Chef Carl Schaubhut, hail from the bayou part of Louisiana (the Cajun coast), and they try to recreate that sensibility in the city. Those low-lying marshy areas, teaming with life in the different species making their homes in the brackish water, have given rise to the dominating Cajun and Creole cultures of the region. Here, the menu reinterprets traditional Cajun food with a lighter touch and more intense flavor. Cajun food is naturally farm to table, as is the food at DTB. There is a lot of seafood and seasonal farm vegetables. Chef Schaubhut sharpened his cooking skills at both Commander's Palace and Café Adelaide before going on to open bacobar in Covington and DTB—his dream restaurant come true in downtown New Orleans.

The restaurant is located in the Riverbend area, where there is a lot of foot traffic. It's a great location for lunch or dinner after a lazy streetcar ride. DTB feels like a special place with interesting decor and a really fun menu. It is very booth oriented, making it feel like private space inside of a crowded restaurant. The back wall of the bar, all penny tiles, takes your eye all the way into the kitchen. The decor is full of found objects, natural things, and curiosities. It is an interesting way to feel that the kitchen is open, but not obtrusive. The squash blossoms are stuffed with an alligator chorizo. That alone is interesting, but it is topped with sauce piquant. This is unusual as just a sauce, but the flavors go together as a constructed whole.

Expect boudin balls, duck, gumbo, crawfish, and oyster. There is cornbread, beef, fish, and lamb. Ice cream sandwiches and pot de crème are sweet finishes to the meal. The food is served with so much pleasure by the wait staff, it's as if the owners have made such a happy place to work that diners get to experience the pleasant atmosphere,

Left: 24-hour short rib. Credit: Max Cusimano.
Right: Brown butter old fashioned. Credit: Max Cusimano.

too. Those who want vegetarian food—often impossible to find at a Cajun or Cajun-inspired restaurant—will find hope at DTB. Flavor rules supreme in a traditional Cajun restaurant, and that applies to the vegetable dishes, too. The rillettes, usually a fat-cooked meat, are made from cauliflower and Brie cheese. You will find ample use of tofu and other surprising ingredients on the menu, but all respectful of Cajun flavors, techniques, and presentation.

There are some house cocktails, but also a knowledgeable bar staff who can create traditional cocktails for you, if you have a favorite. Even here, tradition is expanded and explored. For example, the bar makes use of pecan oil, Peychaud bitters, and other such ingredients in new and interesting ways. There are beers (Louisiana brewed) and wines, with many wines available by the glass. And when eating alone, the bar is a welcoming place for a hungry diner who wants a restaurant experience. The restaurant is open for brunch from Friday through Sunday. Otherwise, it is open daily for happy hour at 4 p.m. and for dinner.

8201 Oak St.
New Orleans, LA
504-518-6889
dtbnola.com

CARMO

The worldwide tropics in New Orleans

New Orleans has been called the northern-most part of the Caribbean. The food eaten here is almost tropical in some of its flavors. That makes it easy to accept the food of the tropics as presented by Carmo, with its Caribbean, South American, Southeast Asian, and West African influences. Dana and Christina Honn are the people behind the Carmo concept. It's an interesting balance between using local and sustainable seafood and other products, and the use of ingredients, flavors, and techniques from around the world.

Dana is an American supporter of the cultural scene and a passionate advocate for sustainable fish. His wife, Christina, was born in Brazil. She is the chef and has put together the menu. She brings to the restaurant the flavors of Brazil, creating a wonderful blend of these two Carnival-loving cultures. The couple opened the restaurant in 2010 and have expanded year by year with new art, community space, and a bar. It has become an anchor in the warehouse district and the go-to place for those who want great, clean food.

One of the hallmarks of Carmo is the freshness of its fish. It has a raw seafood menu as well as quick-cured fish in the Japanese style (sashimi) and tiradito—a Peruvian form of sashimi. The Green Restaurant Association has awarded Carmo the only 3-star rating in the state of Louisiana. It's also certified by Seafood Watch.

The atmosphere at Carmo is friendly and attractive. A series of small rooms give the restaurant a sense of intimacy even when the restaurant is full of activity. It is a place where its commitment to excellent ingredients and its respect for the needs of the diner all come together to produce excellent food, friendly service, and innovative and satisfying flavors. The restaurant is casual, as is the service. This is an excellent choice for parties that are partly vegan, vegetarian, or omnivore. The flavor is never sacrificed when avoiding meat, fish, and dairy products.

Jaciara's Salpicão is a Brazilian chicken salad. It includes chicken, smoked turkey breast, and ham, mixed with raisins, cucumbers, peas, and other vegetables, with a house dressing on greens. Open-faced sandwiches begin with Havarti cheese and scallions as the base. The Creole version adds shrimp, bell peppers, and tomatoes. The maqaquito takes it sweeter with banana and cinnamon sugar.

The dinner menu includes the raw fish plates. Besides the salads that are available at lunch, salads include a Burmese tea leaf salad with fermented tea leaves, cabbage, chiles, tomatoes, and peanuts, with ground shrimp. Miang kham is a sort of salad of spinach leaves, ginger, lime, peanut, and coconut, with bamboo worms, mushrooms, or dried shrimp. The array of dishes from around the world is really comprehensive—the food comes from Sri Lanka, Brazil, and Puerto Rico.

Entrées include a daily curry, a daily rice and beans dish, and a daily special. Desserts include cookies and a Caribbean banana cake, as well as other desserts that are chosen for that day.

Carmo has a bar program that is just as full of fresh tastes as the rest of the menu. The available spirits reflect the tropical panoply. The house cocktails are innovative, although the bar is able to make traditional cocktails. The wine list is adequate and interesting. There are many wines available by the glass, and the beers are equally interesting.

527 Julia St.
New Orleans, LA
504-875-4132
cafecarmo.com

BOURBON HOUSE

Seafood and Bourbon can't go wrong

The concept of *lagniappe,* giving just a little extra to each customer with a purchase, may have fallen by the wayside in most modern cities. Not so in New Orleans, where you might find an extra sprig of herbs you didn't order with your vegetables or a thirteenth roll in a dozen, and definitely not at any of Dickie Brennan's restaurants. At Bourbon House, that Creole way of going above and beyond to charm the customers extends from the raw bar to the dessert menu, to make for an unforgettable experience.

Bourbon House, sitting right there on Bourbon Street, is a restaurant with a double meaning. Yes, it is a restaurant on Bourbon Street, so why not call it Bourbon House? And it's a restaurant that uses bourbon as its theme. There are regular bourbon dinners with special pairings and tastings, often with master distillers explaining the drinks. These are a wonderful experience, and you should check the Bourbon House website to see if one is scheduled. You can join the New Orleans Bourbon Society (NOBS) while you're there and receive a passport and complimentary pour of the bourbon of the month. And because Dickie Brennan wanted a seafood restaurant, why not combine this great Southern spirit with Louisiana seafood?

The bar boasts about 250 types of American spirits, many of them bourbons. This is the place to find those special craft bourbons that you can't find anywhere else. It's a wonderful place to come taste a few different spirits to find the ones that you want to buy for your home bar.

Bourbon House has a fine raw bar. The place is decorated with a collection of interesting oyster plates, some fine and others fun. You

Bourbon Street is not named for the spirits. It is named for the French House of Bourbon, the royal family name of the king of France when the city was founded by the French in 1718.

Left: Bourbon bottles.
Right: Redfish on the half shell.

can also order a tiered fruits de mer, which includes freshly shucked oysters served with Louisiana caviar, boiled shrimp, crab claws, and other available seafood. Appetizers include shrimp calas, a traditional rice fritter, Louisiana sausage, red beans and rice stuffed greens, and crab cakes. The entrées are also very seafood forward. There's a traditional fried seafood platter that's better shared, because it's very generous. Gulf shrimp, catfish, and oyster platters are also available, if you like your seafood one at a time. The bourbon surf and turf, the redfish on the half shell, and the seafood sampler amplify the seafood menu, which also includes a catch of the day, depending on what Gulf fish is available. Of course there's also pasta, jambalaya with roasted chicken, and pork tenderloin for the landlubbers. Bourbon House also serves breakfast. It has a crabcake Benedict, given a similar treatment as their Bourbon House Benedict, served with a blanket of Hollandaise sauce. There are plenty of breakfast temptations and a breakfast buffet.

Desserts include a skillet cobbler with seasonal fruit. There is, as you would expect, a good bit of bourbon in the including bourbon bread pudding, bourbon-soaked corn cake, and even the milk and cookies come with a bourbon milk punch for dunking. The whole menu deserves its own write up, but you've probably gotten the picture by now.

144 Bourbon St.
New Orleans, LA
504-522-0111
bourbonhouse.com

VACHERIE

A bit of Cajun country and Cajun food in the French Quarter

The town of Vacherie is located in the heart of the prairie Cajun country. The name is based on the plains and fields on which the Cajuns raised cattle (*vache*). The Cajuns used the Mississippi River to transport cattle north and south in Louisiana. South of Vacherie is the Lac des Allemands, which leads to the bayous of south Louisiana, the home of the bayou Cajuns. The restaurant Vacherie also touches both the prairie and the bayous in its offerings.

Start your day at Vacherie with a crawfish frittata, with eggs, grits or potatoes, and cheese. The special Cajun sausage, Andouille, made of hand-cut and smoked pork butt, is made into a Cajun hash. Boudin, the liver and rice sausage that is the famous sausage of Cajun land, forms the basis of an eggs Benedict on the Vacherie menu. There is house-made granola and many other goodies.

Dinner at Vacherie is a deeper look into the Cajun table. Fried green tomatoes, chicken biscuits, a plate of Cajun sausages for the table, crabcakes, shrimp, and fried oysters, are just a short listing of the appetizers available at Vacherie. It is absolutely possible to make a delightful meal entirely out of appetizers for the table. The food here is distinctly Cajun, in the French Quarter, but not kitschy or fake. Chef Jarred Zeringue, who first developed the restaurant, made sure of that.

If you would like an entrée, shrimp étouffée and gumbo are great starters. Shrimp and grits, chicken and waffles, pork tenderloin, a pecan chicken, and flatiron steak all make the mouth water. Don't

> The original name of the town Vacherie is *Tabiscanja*, a Colapissa Indian word for long river view. It is located on the west bank of the Mississippi River.

Left: Chalkboard.

Top right: Vacherie interior.

Bottom right: Coffee at Vacherie.

miss the collard greens, yams, or sandwiches, including the Vacherie hamburger. The cheeseburger is served with cheese, bacon, and house-made pickles. If you want a big salad, you can have that, too. The fried oyster salad is a real winner. Shrimp and crabmeat salad is delightful and light. And the Cobb salad is fresh and an unexpected turn on this traditional salad.

There is an adequate wine list, which serves many wines by the glass. The beer list is also well appointed, and this is important when drinking while eating Cajun food because beer often cuts the spice better than wine. Of course, the bar can make any cocktail that you may desire.

827 Toulouse St.
New Orleans, LA
504-207-4532
vacherierestaurant.com

PÊCHE SEAFOOD GRILL

Live-fired fish and more fish

The tradition of live-fire cooking has been enhancing cuisine from around the world for generations. Argentina uses the open-air parilla to grill beef and all its sides. Spain boasts the campfire-style paella to cook its signature rice, rabbit, and chicken dish of the same name. And the Gulf Coast brings the tradition of open hearths to the purist's preparation of the freshest fish and seafood. Inspired by all of these traditions, the founders of Pêche brought them together in this innovative grill. They were able to install an open fire pit right inside the kitchen, and the results are out of this world.

Because of the fire roasting done right in the restaurant, the fish is a far cry from the traditional dishes like trout amandine and trout meunière. Rather, the fare here takes a rustic preparation style to the freshest local ingredients to create contemporary masterpieces. There is a raw bar where you can get everything from raw oysters to steak tartare with oyster aioli. Shrimp toast and hushpuppies can be eaten by themselves or shared at the table.

Chef Ryan Prewitt, Pêche's chef, was recognized by the James Beard Foundation for Best Chef in the South, and Pêche was named Best New Restaurant in America in 2014. The Pêche founders were looking to explore cooking whole fish and whole anything in fire. They struggled to create the right open fire environment in the middle of the city, but the struggle was worth it. And they took a chance with their vision. This is as far from a traditional New Orleans seafood restaurant as you can get. Even the seasoning is not what the New Orleanian is used to. But everything at Pêche is truly delicious.

If you're a bit hungrier, you can get gumbo, lamb, or grilled chicken. And that's important to know if not everyone in your party is in the mood for seafood. It turns out that cooking over a live fire works just as well for lamb and chicken as it does for fish. But be prepared for some

Left: Ground shrimp noodles.
Right: Key lime.

wonderful transformations of fish. While you're there, take a minute to watch the food and fire.

If you want to share, try the whole grilled fish, big enough for several eaters. Depending on your sides, you can stretch that fish to four or five eaters. There's also an enormous ribeye for sharing. It starts out at least twenty-two ounces before grilling. Beets, fried Brussels sprouts, beans, and riced cauliflower can complete your meal.

The desserts are sweet, but the two salted dishes—salted peanut butter pie and salted caramel cake—let you ease into dessert from the savory meal. The bar program and wines are good accompaniments to the dinner.

Pêche has a strong bar program and a nice wine and beer list. Small plates at the bar make for a pleasant way to have a late afternoon meeting.

800 Magazine St.
New Orleans, LA
504-522-1744
pecherestaurant.com

THE GRILL ROOM AT WINDSOR COURT

Dining for the Anglophile

The hunting pictures, dog portraits, and other English touchstones on the walls give you the first taste of this Anglophile jewel in the luxurious Windsor Court Hotel. The Grill Room dovetails perfectly with the impeccably curated English theme of the hotel, and it invites its guests to enjoy the finer points of the dining experience from across the pond. Upstairs, the cozier Polo Club Lounge builds on the theme with more traditional pub fare, like fish and chips, within an atmosphere meant to honor the traditional English hunt club.

Why would you want to eat in a restaurant in a hotel? Because Jimmy Coleman, the Anglophile who opened the Windsor Court as a distinctly English type of hotel, made sure that the elegant approach to the hotel would also be reflected in its restaurant. The decor is English, with hundreds of paintings depicting the British countryside and with tea and other specialties served at breakfast. The lunch and nightly fare are prepared by four-star chefs. It's not the typical food of New Orleans, but it is consistently superb.

Breakfast includes fruits—notable is the brûléed grapefruit—and granola and yogurt combinations. A continental breakfast with pastries of various kinds allows for a light breakfast. Eggs, waffles, pancakes, French toast, and beignets are offered as well.

The dinner menu is much more elegant than breakfast, which is delicious, but more businesslike. Dinner is very luxe. It includes foie gras, seared yellow fin tuna, and steak. The Grill Room crab cake is served with a remoulade, scallop crudo, and both sea bass and redfish. Pappardelle and lamb ragu with cilantro, sumac, and ricotta and beef carpaccio with olive oil, quail egg, and Parmesan cheese are

Left: Coulotte steak and eggs.
Right: Duck breast dinner.

also available as appetizers along with gnocchi with sage and truffle shavings. In addition, a salad of beets and citrus with hearts of palm on frisée adds an interesting, fresh option. The Caesar salad is served with fried anchovies and Manchego cheese.

As for dessert there's a banana bread pudding served with a brûléed banana and butterscotch spread. Also on offer is a lemon cheesecake with almond crumble and strawberry compote. A chocolate cake with a chocolate and raspberry mousse with a passion fruit sauce is one of the more decadent dishes. There's also a triple brûlée —chocolate hazelnut, lemon, and coffee.

Weekends mean brunch with music at the Windsor Court and the Grill Room. The breakfast menu is expanded to include shrimp and grits, stuffed beignets, and eggs Atchafalaya. The mimosa is offered for brunch celebration. Having received the 2018 *Wine Spectator* award of excellence, the wine list is quite extensive, with many wines available by the glass. The wine list is updated online regularly, so if your interest is fine wines, check the website before making a reservation.

300 Gravier St.
New Orleans, LA
504-522-1994
grillroomneworleans.com

CAFÉ BEIGNET

There is more than one place to eat a beignet

The delicious treats at Café Beignet are synonymous with another New Orleans delicacy: jazz music. That's because their Bourbon Street location is also set within a public park, Musical Legends Park, where Steamboat Willie and his jazz band take the stage every night. The sounds of their horns and saxophones float through the quaint park, studded with bronze statues of legends of the trade like Fats Domino and Allen Toussaint. There's no cover charge, no drink minimum, and no exclusion. This is jazz music the way it was first invented right here in the 1920s. The concert is not a hackneyed review of all the commonly recognized jazz pieces, but rather a musical presentation in the manner of the old period of jazz and tunes that reflect that era.

Though you don't have to buy a drink or a sweet treat to enjoy along with your jazz, Café Beignet is the perfect spot to do so to complete the experience. Especially if you want to try its signature dish—New Orleans's beloved beignet. The line at Café du Monde can be very long, however a trip to one of the locations of Café Beignet can fill the bill if you have a hankering to taste those lovely pillows of powdered sugar on fried dough. There's no yeast in these fluffy pastries. Instead, they're like a choux pastry that gets its rise from the steam created inside as it fries. The beignets come three to an order, which is the tradition in the city. Eat them quickly because they are best hot. Of course, you can always get a beignet, but at Café Beignet you have a few more protein options, like an omelette, waffles, scrambled eggs, a breakfast croissant, or bagel.

You can also get other traditional foods at Café Beignet. That means red beans and rice, various po'boys, jambalaya, and gumbo. Fried seafood platters are also available and are a good choice if you're hungry. You should also try some of the specialty cocktails that are

The greats in the courtyard.

available, many of them eye openers like a spicy Bloody Mary or a mint julep. A traditional Sazerac would also be a good choice.

Besides coffee to accompany your beignet, there are many fountain drink choices, iced coffee, including a mocha, lemonade, juices, milk, and iced tea. There are three locations of Café Beignet and they are all in the French Quarter.

311 Bourbon St.
334 Royal St.
600 Decatur St.
cafebeignet.com

AMERICAN SECTOR RESTAURANT & BAR

Elevated museum fare for the discerning visitor

Food is everywhere in New Orleans and the bar is set high for good food at restaurants, even when you least expect it. For example, you'll find a restaurant full of good food at the National World War II Museum.

Far from standard museum fare, American Sector is a real restaurant that reflects the city, not just a place to fill up in between galleries at the museum. Whether you're stopping in for a civilized bite before resuming your visit, or sitting down for a proper meal, it will be worth it.

Open for lunch and dinner every day, with Saturday and Sunday brunch, American Sector offers an array of playfully named dishes that deliver on flavor. Bugle Call, Admiral's Crabbie Patties, and Sargent's Sardou do not disappoint. The food and ambiance are very child friendly, making eating at American Sector easy for visitors of all ages. You can chow down on a Fort Bragg Dog, southern favorites like shrimp and grits, and homey comfort foods like meatloaf. The restaurant is walled with glass on the street side, making the diners feel as though they are outside. And the front window wall can be retracted for unique al fresco dining.

American Sector is great for a meal, but if you want just a snack, the Soda Shop offers real old-fashioned sodas, sandwiches, and other soda fountain fare. And if you are in the mood for a World War II-era dinner and a show, try the Stage Door Canteen. The show is always changing, so check for what is playing before you go.

Left: Shrimp Louis Armstrong.

Right: Dining by the windows.

Cocktails here are named as playfully as the food. G.I. Punch and Rosemary Riveter keep the mood light, and all are as tasty as they are imaginative.

Worried that you don't have time to visit the museum and experience American Sector? Fear not. The restaurant is open to all and even stays open beyond the museum's hours, so everyone can stop in for a taste.

1035 Magazine St.
New Orleans, LA
504-528-1940
ww2eats.com

LUVI

Shanghai comfort food with a Japanese twist

One of chef/owner Hao Gong's beliefs is that you first begin to taste food with your eyes, even before your mouth. It's that kind of attention to the full sensory experience that has helped him adapt every part of the culinary journey at Luvi. Taste begins as you walk in the doors of the small restaurant and take in the explosion of colors and patterns that make up the decor. The small space should feel even smaller because of the clash of patterns, but the choices were so precisely unusual and right, that the restaurant feels larger instead of smaller. The interior design is the creation of the chef's wife, Jennifer Wade, and it supports the intended effect of open-minded dining.

Next, your attention turns to the carefully curated menu of primarily Chinese dishes with Japanese notes. Chef Gong has created a menu full of whimsically named dishes that reflect his idea of comfort food from Shanghai. You'd probably never guess the contents of each dish by its name, which adds to the fun. The food is serious, however, and comes to your table with a thoughtfulness about taste.

You'll probably start with the raw menu, which is just as extensive as the other offerings. For seafood lovers, it's a testament to the freshness of the fish. Snow White, the ceviche made with whitefish, also includes Rice Krispies. The red and green Stoplight is made with yellowtail and jalapeño. And Under the Sea, a raw mixed seafood salad with a jalapeño lemon aioli, changes with the season.

The small plates are not really small, but they are tasty. Lion's Head is crab and a pork meatball served in bone broth. Dark Forest is fried tofu with wild mushrooms. The medium plates are also part of the clever names theme. The Happy Meal is a caramelized ginger soy chicken. Stolen Treasure is baked salmon, truffle oil with a sweet soy reduction. And Happy Buddha is a pan-seared white fish with shitake and portobello mushrooms with fried leeks. And there are also noodles, such as the Spicy Dan Dan Noodles with chicken, black beans, and

Left: Interior shot—all color and fun.
Right: Lion's Head. Credit: Sam Hanna.

ghost chili oil. On the side, try the Five Scented Edamame, a spring roll with pork and cabbage, or a smashed cucumber salad with garlic and soy vinegar.

The restaurant presents its own cocktails, which are as clever in their names as their ingredients. Luvi Lychee is a martini that is made with sake and lychee. The Blue Uzumaki is another sake cocktail that is a riff on a mojito, with pomegranate liqueur and blueberries. The list of sakes is long for a New Orleans restaurant and establishes the premise that sakes are varied and nuanced. It warrants many visits to establish a bit of understanding of those flavors. Besides the cocktails, which are a surprising and delicious beginning to a meal at Luvi, there are wines by the bottle and by the glass. And there is a lychee wine and Japanese plum wines.

Having trouble deciding with so many interesting and diverse choices? Chef Gong also offers two "Feed Me" options. These are meals left to the chef's discretion, based on what is best that day. With an open mind, you're sure to enjoy the experience from sight to taste and beyond.

5236 Tchoupitoulas St.
New Orleans, LA
504-601-3340
luvirestaurant.com

EAT NEW ORLEANS

A tiny gem in the residential corner of the French Quarter

In a quiet corner of the French Quarter sits the tiny neighborhood restaurant, Eat. You could almost pass right by the charming and sunny space, mistaking it for a home on this residential corner, but you'll be sorry if you do. After Hurricane Katrina, local chef Jarred Zeringue was determined to create a restaurant that would help preserve the food and culture of the city and Louisiana. He wanted a place to serve farm fresh food in the tradition of the dishes he had grown up eating and loving. EAT New Orleans was born from this desire.

The restaurant is open at lunch and dinner, with an ever-changing menu. This restaurant serves fresh Louisiana favorites and many family recipes, made with traditional ingredients the bulk of which are farmed or produced locally. Chef Jarred and other owners of the restaurant also own Wayne Jacobs Smokehouse in LaPlace, where they make traditional sausages like Andouille and smoked sausage without preservatives. The gumbos and other Louisiana dishes benefit from that locally made and controlled charcuterie.

The menu contains many country Louisiana favorites, like figs, hog's head cheese, and chicken livers with pepper jelly. Shrimp and beans as well as gumbo are traditionally presented to make your meal feel

About thirty-five miles outside of New Orleans you can find Wayne Jacobs Smokehouse. It supplies eggs, tasso, and Andouille to EAT. If you can make the trip, try the Smokehouse for lunch. The deviled eggs, using fresh eggs from the chickens out back, are delicious. The gumbo and biscuits are outstanding. If you're inclined to take food home, look for the pickles, house-made hot sauce, and smoked duck and rabbit for sale at the Smokehouse.

Decadent bananas.

homey. It's a place with lots of regulars, because they know what it means to find a consistent restaurant that makes you feel like you are eating in your mother's kitchen, only better. Blue-plate specials like crawfish pie and fried chicken just continue to underscore the theme. The restaurant is far from vegan, but if you are looking for vegetarian options, the menu is full of them. They are all tasty and not designed to make you aware that something is missing, because nothing is. And to continue to preserve the entire culture, the work of local artists is hanging on the walls.

There is something for everyone. Don't miss the Brussels sprout salad, and, if you are inclined, there is a black-eyed pea burger. Baked macaroni and cheese and smashed potatoes just make you smile. Desserts are house made and, while ever changing, complete the theme of country meals served at EAT.

900 Dumaine St.
New Orleans, LA
504-522-7222
eatnola.com

CHARLIE'S STEAKHOUSE AND BAR

An old-fashioned steakhouse in old uptown

For over eighty years, people in New Orleans have been eating at Charlie's Steakhouse on Dryades Street. It is a quintessentially New Orleans restaurant, and any tourists that you see are definitely in the know. Without a doubt, this is a steak house. The T-bone steak could serve as dinner for three—it weighs two pounds! There's also New York strip, filet, and ribeye. But as steakhouses go, this secret New Orleans restaurant is a bargain. There's no attempt to do everything here; it's a no-frills steakhouse. And by no frills, I mean there aren't lots of other choices. It's worth the trip, but if you want something other than a steak, don't bother.

Charlie's has been serving steaks since 1932, making it the oldest steakhouse in the city. It was founded by Charlie Petrossi in a city where steak is prepared with the same reverence as seafood. Charlie is credited with using a hot metal platter to keep sizzling steaks hot. People come from all over the city to eat there, knowing what they want without a menu. Everyone relies on the servers to let them know what is available that day.

Traditional appetizers include fried onion rings piled high on the plate, mushrooms Bordelaise, French onion soup, and a classic crabmeat au gratin. The place looks old school, and it is. The lettuce in the salads is iceberg. The dressings that can be poured over the lettuce wedge are thick, delicious, and house made. The restaurant serves many types of potatoes, so it's not necessary to settle for mashed or baked potatoes, and there are large cut fries. Quite a few vegetable choices make for sides like broccoli and other fresh vegetables, peas, mushrooms, spinach, asparagus, and dishes with and without cheese. There is also a tuna steak available for those who want another type of choice.

Top: Charlie's at night.
Left: Gracious and friendly service.

The restaurant definitely feels like a place from another time. The meat is aged prime beef. And the desserts are also old school. They are gelati and ices from Angelo Brocato's with flavors like spumoni, pistachio, torroncino, and biscotti from the old Sicilian bakery. There is a full wine list to pair with your steak, with many wines available by the glass, and beer, and spirits.

4510 Dryades St.
New Orleans, LA
504-895-9323
charliessteakhouse.com

AVO

A modern Italian restaurant

What are called Italian restaurants in New Orleans are very often really Creole Italian restaurants. They are good, but they're not really a taste of Italy. They usually serve overly sauced pasta and in New Orleans serve red gravy—a roux-based sauce—instead of tomato sauce. Avo is an exception. The flavors and techniques are truly Italian. However, in spite of not serving the traditional food of New Orleans, the restaurant still feels like a restaurant in New Orleans—you'll know it by its welcoming atmosphere.

Nick Lama is of Italian descent, but he didn't learn to cook in Italy. Somehow he still brings that ancestral sensibility to his food, having learned to cook in the family kitchen with his mother and his grandmother. The pasta, the sauces, and the condiments are all house made. Chef Lama has appeared on NBC's *Today* to share his family's recipes, especially on St. Joseph Day, when those of Italian (specifically, Sicilian) descent visit altars throughout the city to honor St. Joseph. He has won many accolades with Avo, and one of the most important is having been named the Italian Restaurant of the Year in 2015 by *New Orleans* magazine. In keeping with the Sicilian tradition, this restaurant is a family affair that includes Chef Nick's wife, Melissa, and other family members.

The restaurant is not open for lunch, so go for Saturday or Sunday brunch or dinner. The menu is heavy with traditional Italian seafood

Chef Lama's family hails from Sicily. His grandfather and his father ran the St. Roch Market on St. Claude Avenue before Hurricane Katrina. They supplied the neighborhood with fresh fish and a famous gumbo, which they sold by the gallon. Chef Lama has made the competitive cooking circuit on TV appearing on Bravo's *Top Chef Masters.*

Avo's interior.

like octopus and calamari. Other familiar and traditional dishes include stuffed zucchini blossoms, scallops, and a variety of pasta. Everything—including the desserts—makes you feel that you are eating in Italy. Avo is a modern Italian restaurant, both in its look and on the table, but there is nothing boring or predictable about it. It feels as though the restaurant is interpreting the food in a forward way and not in the back-looking way of so many Italian restaurants on this side of the Atlantic.

The food at Avo is intensely seasoned. That does not mean hot; it means intense. Intense flavors is a very New Orleans concept. So using a modern Italian sensibility, Avo presents modern food that uses avocados, lobster, risotto, rabbit, ribs, and even carrots to create and underscore flavor.

The restaurant has an indoor section and a great, enclosed patio that feels like a protected outdoors. The roof actually retracts, so when the weather is right, that is the place to be. And in true Italian tradition, there aren't lots of dessert choices. The panna cotta is silky. The wine list is not very deep, but it is adequate. It's full of Italian wines, which find a cozy fit with the items on the menu.

5909 Magazine St.
New Orleans, LA
504-509-6550
restaurantavo.com

MONDO

World flavor in the suburbs

Chef Susan Spicer's casual restaurant in Lakeview, Mondo, is a simple neighborhood place whose food is always good. Chef Spicer has ensured that the attention to detail that she applies to Bayona, her white tablecloth French Quarter restaurant, is applied to Mondo with the same knowing hand. Mondo is a farm-to-table restaurant, which makes a serious effort to source local products that reflect the chef's interest in international flavors.

Chef Susan Spicer and her family live in Lakeview, so it makes sense to locate Mondo close to home. And it makes sense to want it to be good. As a result of her own upbringing and experience training in restaurants around the world, Chef Spicer wanted to have a place to apply her talents to global cuisine. The restaurant is not called Mondo—which means "world" in Italian—for nothing. The global approach to flavor and ingredients makes the restaurant a special place for a neighborhood restaurant.

Mondo has lots of snacks to enhance a round of drinks, perhaps on the way home from work. The lunch menu is delightful with a burger and sandwiches such as the fried shrimp banh mi, as well as heartier choices. The pizzas are a wonderful informal addition to the menu. Dinnertime is also informal and the burger is still available. But also at night, you can order curried shrimp and cauliflower or broiled Gulf fish. Chicken liver pâté and ceviche are examples of how the menu jumps all over the world.

For desserts there are ice creams and sorbets, chocolate cake, and a pot de crème. There's a lemon tart, and best of all, a root beer float.

The bar program and wine list are broad. The snacks are innovative, such as warm Gorgonzola, smoked trout spread, pimento cheese, and deviled eggs, and can be shared at the table or at the bar. The shrimp and pork meatballs are marvelous. Mussels and pâté make for great

Top: Mondo exterior.

Left: Chef Susan Spicer.

starters. Such sides as Brussels sprouts, fries, and broccoli can make a meal with the starters. And if you're hungry, their shrimp and Szechuan eggplant stir fry, braised short ribs, or a burger may call to you.

900 Harrison Ave.
New Orleans, LA
504-224-2633

UPPERLINE

The city's living room

Brimming with New Orleans hospitality and the flavors of the city, Upperline is a warm and welcoming restaurant in the uptown part of the city. JoAnn Clevenger, recognized by the James Beard Foundation for her hospitality, presides over the dining room at Upperline, making sure that everyone feels at home. It's truly a wonderful place to have a celebratory dinner, even if you're just celebrating being in New Orleans. The walls of the dining room are covered with local art. The restaurant rocks with great conversation and happy people.

JoAnn is not a chef, but she has a talented palate. After a career as a tavern owner and a theater costume designer, JoAnn reinvented herself as a restaurateur. Her restaurant feels like her living room. She presides over the rooms, representing the first floor of an old building, with the grace and hospitality of an old friend. Always the ambassador for New Orleans—complete with a fleur-de-lis pin—she wears her signature color, red. With all the experience she has at costume designing, she knows how to dress and set a stage.

Her restaurant is full of people who have worked for her for a long time—people who have risen up through the ranks from dishwasher to cook. She will tell you about inventing dishes in her dreams and other great stories about food and eating. Eat the fried green tomato shrimp remoulade, one of the dishes JoAnn says she visualized in a dream. The menu includes several generous and filling tasting menus, reflective of traditional Louisiana flavors. The restaurant is known for its treatment of duck, so you cannot go wrong with almost any duck dish. And the cheese, steak, and shrimp are absolutely wonderful. This is the place to send anyone who's looking for a New Orleans experience outside of the French Quarter; a place where locals go.

Top: A complete appetizer.
Right: Surf and turf.

The wine list is excellent, as is the bar. And the assortment of selections that are decidedly postprandial is just the reason to linger after the meal in the warm atmosphere of the place. JoAnn is ready for tourists, however, with a list of places in the city that are not to be missed, which she will gladly pass to you as you leave if you're a visitor to the city. She's sharing her love of good food and a wonderful city with you.

1413 Upperline St.
New Orleans, LA
504-891-9822
upperline.com

CAFÉ DU MONDE

Hot dough and sugar will get you every time

Regardless of the hour, a walk by Café du Monde will mean you are serenaded by the smell of hot oil and sugar. There's not much more satisfying than that hot square of fried pastry dough covered with powdered sugar we call a beignet. It's not just the beignets that call to you from Café du Monde, however, as there are many places to eat a good beignet in the French Quarter. You go there instead for the feel of the place. It's like an old coffee house, especially inside where the very countertops tell stories of the people who have eaten there since 1862. There were once two beignet parlors bookending the French Market, but now there is only one: Café du Monde.

It is so old and well known for its beignets, chicory coffee, and hot chocolate, that there is often a line down the block to have a taste. New Orleanians know that it's open twenty-four hours a day. After prom, a Mardi Gras ball, or any late night event, you can see patrons wearing formal wear—that means a tuxedo or sequined gown covered with powdered sugar by the end of their visit. Just a table away there might be a person down on his luck who scraped together enough change to buy an order of beignets. It's really a New Orleans moment in which all classes coexist peacefully over food. At two or three o'clock in the morning, there is no line. To avoid the lines, make this the last thing you do after a night of listening to jazz. And there are a number of satellite locations around the city. Café du Monde is open every day except Christmas. It's historic and reliable.

Meanwhile Back at Café du Monde. This book, full of food memories and food stories, was the loving brainchild of Peggy Sweeney-McDonald. It chronicles food stories of many people who have great yarns to spin. It demonstrates just how we are all connected by food.

Top: Sugar. Credit: Peggy Sweeney McDonald.

Right: Sign. Credit: Peggy Sweeney McDonald.

You can sit inside at the old counter watching things being made. Or you can sit outside at a table. There are usually pigeons hanging around to scrounge for sweet crumbs. They belong there as much as the people. And if you're really fascinated, you can watch the beignets being prepared through a glass window created just for that purpose. If nothing else entices you in, that will.

800 Decatur St.
New Orleans, LA
504-525-4544
cafedumonde.com

COMMANDER'S PALACE

Elegant dining in the Uptown

Located in the Garden District, Commander's Palace is one of the grand uptown restaurants that has a long legacy serving the families of New Orleans. It was founded by Emile Commander as a small saloon in 1893. Since being purchased by the Brennan family in 1974, Commander's has become known for its special blue exterior paint color. It has garnered numerous James Beard Awards, as well as other awards. It is now operated by the next generation of cousins, Ti Adelaide Martin and Lally Brennan, who call themselves the Cocktail Chicks. Today it is known for its fine dining and excellent service, but with fun touches that keep it from feeling stuffy or pretentious. If you are looking for snooty, this is the wrong place.

Taking a chance on Cajun Chef Paul Prudhomme, who, along with Ella Brennan, shaped the menu into a Louisiana establishment, Commander's Palace began to attract diners who were looking for something a bit different; they transformed the old restaurant into one that serves modern takes on New Orleans food with local ingredients. For example, they stepped away from using almonds, which are not a local product, and now embrace pecans, which are. Now, fish crusted with pecans has become a Commander's classic. Besides establishing the reputation of Prudhomme—who went on to own K-Paul's, write many cookbooks, and develop a long running PBS series—Commander's also gave a start to Emeril Lagasse, the late Jamie Shannon, and current Executive Chef Tory McPhail.

Service at Commander's Palace is world famous. The Commander's signature is to have all of the servers pick up a table's waiting dishes and place the plates in front of guests all at the same time with great flourish. It is very dramatic and lots of fun.

Garden Room.

You can choose a tasting menu rather than ordering à la carte. So many dishes change regularly, it is hard to be too specific, but you can always on a gumbo of some sort on the menu and a turtle soup. Crawfish and buttermilk gnocchi is a good selection. The salads are large and crisply fresh with wonderful cheeses and other added treats. The redfish, quail, and soft-shell crab Rangoon are surefire choices.

The signature dessert is the bread pudding soufflé. It is outstanding. Order it when you order dinner. Don't wait to decide that you want it at the end, or you may be out of luck. It will also help you temper your order, lest you forget to save room for this light and airy soufflé that *Garden and Gun* magazine once called, "one hell of a thing."

The wine list, including dessert wines, is award winning. The cocktail program is top notch, and you will find something to make the pairings at your table very special.

The massive restaurant has a garden room with glass walls that make you feel as if you are eating in the trees. A courtyard and other rooms are entered through the immaculate kitchen. The service is precise and attentive. Everyone is served at the same time. You know from that special service that you are eating at Commander's Palace. A chef's table in the kitchen is often booked by people who want to watch the show in the there while they eat. It is very popular and you must reserve it.

1403 Washington Ave.
New Orleans, LA
504-899-8221
commanderspalace.com

LA BOULANGERIE

A French bakery with a New Orleans twist

The smell of freshly baked bread wafts down every street in France, inviting and mouthwatering. But the term *boulangerie* is reserved only for those establishments that bake their own bread on the premises. These bakeries honor centuries of tradition in baking and infuse their own regional and personal flavors into the loaves they craft. You'll know a good one by the line out the door.

With Executive Pastry Chef Maggie Scales at the helm, that is precisely what the Link Restaurant Group has accomplished on Magazine Street with La Boulangerie. Originally created by Dominique Rizzo with the intention to create authentic French breads, it still retains the French feeling of its origins, now expanding its culinary reach to include that masterpiece of bread: the great sandwich.

La Boulangerie expanded to include not only bread and pastries, but also sandwiches, ice cream, and bagels. The bakery has its whole wheat flour ground by Bellegarde Bakery in New Orleans, indicating the care taken with ingredients. Every day the list of breads always available is large. The bread is available throughout the day. The boules, fougasses, whole-wheat loaves, baguettes and mini baguettes, rye and other breads, bagels, and pretzel knots are always available. The challah is rich and eggy, but only available on Fridays.

The pastries are a mixture of what you would expect and some surprises. The apple frangipane tart is a special treat. Lemon meringue tarts, brownies, eclairs, cookies, and Napoleons are on offer. There are also cakes and pies, such as cheesecake tiramisu, carrot cake, and Black

This place is busy all year, but make sure to stop by during Mardi Gras for its wonderful king cake, different from most king cakes in New Orleans. Theirs is made with laminated dough, so its texture is light and its flavor is delightful.

Ice cream.

Forest cake. The ice creams and sherbets change with the seasons. They are made in house and served in house-made waffle cones.

All of this is wonderful, of course, and it makes La Boulangerie smell wonderful even if you just pass it on the street. But the sandwiches are the real siren call. The breakfast sandwich is presented on a croissant with a spicy egg, cheese, and breakfast sausage. When taken with a cup of coffee, it's a breakfast of champions. The salmon bagel is served with the traditional accompaniments. The chicken salad is served on a croissant with a small salad. That's the kind of lunch that makes you happy in this city. There's always something to eat and being able to have a lighter lunch, quickly prepared, that won't make you feel so full after several days of delicious restaurant eating is a real treat.

Le Dindon, the turkey sandwich with avocado, arugula, and tomato on six-grain bread, is a classic prepared with precision that exceeds expectations. Le Dindon is worth crossing the city for. The ham, salami, and other cured meats are made at Cochon Butcher, a sister restaurant to La Boulangerie within the Link Restaurant Group.

And you can also enjoy buns, muffins, croissants (including the important almond and chocolate kind), turnovers and scones. On the savory side there are kolaches, quiches, pretzels, meat pies, a ham and cheese croissant, and vol au vent. For a place where people still use these flaky pastry shells at home to make dishes or even passed appetizers, this is a welcome offering. Pop in for a quick meal or a snack.

4600 Magazine St.
New Orleans, LA
504-269-3777
laboulangerienola.com

CARROLLTON MARKET (page 6)

K-PAUL'S LOUISIANA KITCHEN (page 116)

SALON BY SUCRÉ (page 40)

Credit: Sam Hanna

BAYONA (page 16)

COMMANDER'S PALACE (page 82)

PYTHIAN MARKET (page 130)

MAYPOP (page 22)

BOURBON HOUSE (page 56)

DICKIE BRENNAN'S STEAKHOUSE (page 104)

RALPH'S ON THE PARK (page 176)

ANDREA'S (page 36)

BRENNAN'S (page 30)

GOMPÈRE LAPIN (page 180)

ANGELO BROCATO ORIGINAL ITALIAN ICE CREAM PARLOR (page 124)

BEACHBUM BERRY'S LATITUDE 29 (page 144)

PALACE CAFÉ (page 178)

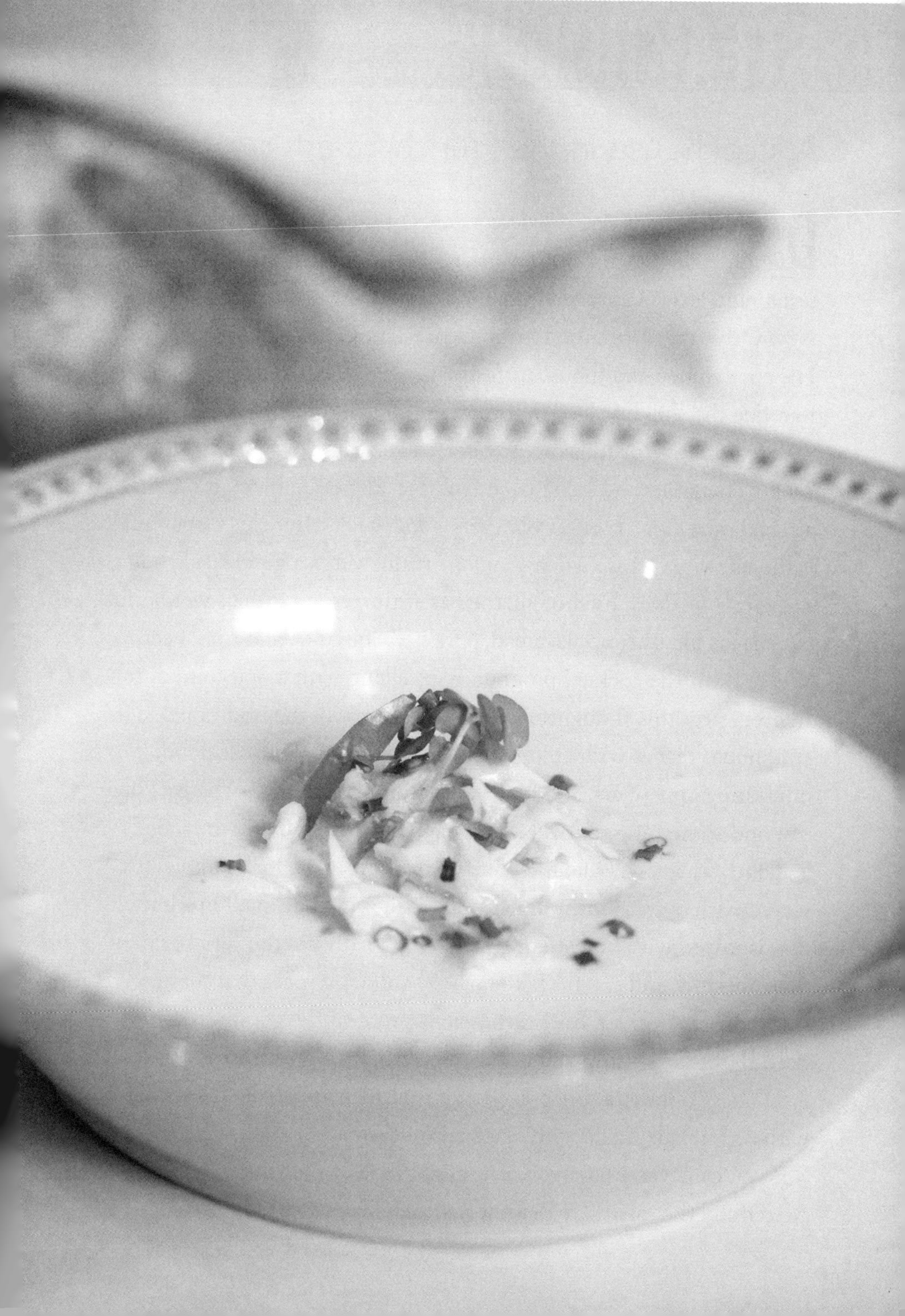

DAKOTA (page 152)

DICKIE BRENNAN'S STEAKHOUSE

A steakhouse in the French Quarter

Dickie Brennan is one the descendants of the distinguished Brennan family—famous for restaurants, food, and service. He opened this restaurant, as well as several others, to honor the great culinary legacy of New Orleans by bringing top-quality restaurants to the French Quarter. His eponymous steakhouse turns the focus to meat and continuing to refine the skill involved in its proper preparation. Dickie has said, "We're not here for today, we're here for 50 years down the road."

Don't be fooled—Dickie Brennan's Steakhouse is much more than a steakhouse. Yes, it serves very, very good steaks. But this restaurant is the one you choose when someone really wants a good steak, but not everyone does. First of all, the bar at the restaurant has wonderful bar snacks like shrimp flatbread, pork belly biscuits, and mini beef Wellington. The cocktail program is excellent, with a nod to tradition. In every way, this thoughtful restaurant serves up the traditional steakhouse dishes with aplomb, but also prepares lots of seafood, interesting appetizers, and fun desserts so that everyone who eats here can find something to make them happy. The richness of the menu is mouth watering. Take the bone marrow escargot, for example. It's served with oyster mushrooms, leeks, garlic, and bacon all in a butter that is mixed with bone marrow. There is hardly anything richer than bone marrow, and it reflects the whole-animal respect that too few steakhouses consider. Beef carpaccio is proof of the goodness of the beef. Barbecue shrimp and grits is a Southern/New Orleans combo. And my goodness, a foie gras biscuit is also an appetizer. It's served with a gastrique made with seasonal fruit.

If you can even imagine it, you might look at the salads and soups. Mercifully the salads are definitely steakhouse standards. A wedge of

Left: Chateaubriand. Credit: Sara Essex Bradley.
Right: Sweet potato doberge.

iceberg, burrata, and tomato or a Caesar can serve as a crisp and fresh contrast against a steak. Soups are either turtle soup or a changing gumbo. Potatoes are available in the usual steakhouse manner, with the addition of a roasted sweet potato. The sides are also very standard, not in flavor, but in choices like macaroni and cheese, green beans, spinach, sautéed vegetables, onion rings, and roasted corn.

All of the standard cuts of beef are available. In addition, you can order half of a roasted chicken served with alligator sauce piquant. Grilled Gulf fish is available, as well as barbecue ribeye. Steak and oysters are available, and so are lobster, pork belly, and scallops.

If you still have room in your belly, you should try the coconut cake. There's also a traditional crème brûlée and a bananas Foster cheesecake. The bread pudding is called French toast bread pudding, served with whiskey syrup and pecans.

The bar menu is very rich and meaty, too, and the bar program itself is definitely a place to enjoy your palate. The cheese board and fries will sustain you while you drink. The bar has great cocktails and also mocktails for those who want to imbibe without an impact.

716 Iberville St.
New Orleans, LA
504-522-2467
dickiebrennanssteakhouse.com

NAPOLEON HOUSE

The place where an exiled emperor *almost* stayed

A building can be historically significant for what didn't happen there, just as it can for what did. When Napoleon Bonaparte faced exile from France, he found many sympathizers in the North American territories that had been part of the Louisiana Purchase—including Louisiana and, thus, New Orleans. Though they had become part of the newly minted United States, there were many people of French descent there still very attached to their motherland.

One such sympathizer was the mayor of New Orleans, Nicholas Girod; modern city dwellers will recognize his name from the street named in his honor in the Central Business District. As mayor, he prepared his own home to receive the exiled Napoleon, who died before he could ever find refuge in New Orleans. Nevertheless, the house was forever known as the place that anticipated the arrival of Napoleon. To this day, the Napoleon House is very much fascinated by the former emperor, and it plays the Eroica symphony, which Beethoven originally wrote to honor Napoleon.

Napoleon House is a casual dining establishment where the bar is just as important as the food, in keeping with the tradition of New Orleans. The specialty of the house is the muffuletta. This specialty was established by the Impastato family, who owned the restaurant and bar for many decades. They have always honored the building's place in New Orleans history, as do the current owners. The muffuletta is made

> The Pimm's cup was not invented in New Orleans, but in the mid-twentieth century it became very popular there. It's a gin-based drink with lemonade and lemon/lime soda, garnished with a cucumber slice.

Muffuletta.

with ham, Genoa salami, pastrami, Swiss cheese, provolone, and a generous amount of house-made olive salad. Distinguishing itself from Central Grocery—which claims to have invented the muffuletta—Napoleon House serves the sandwich warm. This is a very special sandwich, which is tall and thick, and that thick bread absorbs the olive oil from the olive salad. The cheese melts and adds a wonderful texture to the entire sandwich. Some have been tempted to eat it with a knife and fork, but it's meant to be picked up by hand.

The shrimp remoulade served in an avocado is a wonderful and light alternative to the muffuletta. The Caesar salad is a good accompaniment to any lunch. And the gumbo is tasty, too. A cheese board and a charcuterie board are both wonderful to share and go well with drinks or as a snack. Mondays are the traditional day for red beans and rice in New Orleans, but if you're hungry for them anytime, this is the place. The jambalaya is tasty and spicy. The restaurant serves a turkey club sandwich and a grilled alligator sausage po'boy. The desserts are few but classic: bread pudding, cannoli, and fruit.

The bar is well known for the Pimm's cup, its signature drink. Besides the original, the bar also has two additional variations—the English Pimm's and the Ponchatoula Pimm's. The Margarita in Exile is a variation of the classic drink with Mandarin Napoleon. And the other drinks are very classic, as would be expected in a place so steeped in history. Of course there is wine and beer to complete the bar selections.

500 Chartres St.
New Orleans, LA
504-524-9752
napoleonhouse.com

REVEL CAFÉ & BAR

Cocktails from a true historian

If you like a little history lesson with your drink, the place to go is Revel. Award-winning bartender and co-founder of the Museum of the American Cocktail, Chris McMillian will make you traditional cocktails and tell you the history behind them. His mint julep is state of the art, especially when it's accompanied by the poetry that Chris may choose to recite as he makes it. *Imbibe* magazine named Chris as one of the most influential cocktail personalities of the twentieth century. Sitting at the bar upstairs is the friendliest place to be if you are alone. Chris is such a great storyteller, you will feel welcome and in good company.

The bar food is simple and satisfying in the downstairs dining room—cheese and meat plates, house-pickled vegetables, and fries. It is a satisfying place to enjoy the traditions of New Orleans. The Sazerac, old-fashioned, or manhattan will transport you to an older time in the city when bars served lunch. The food at Revel is more than just bar food. The breads are homemade and full of variety. Those fresh breads make the sandwiches more than bread and filler. The sandwiches are remarkable and just as well crafted and well thought out as the cocktails.

The wines list is also quite extensive at Revel, and they have a nice selection of beers. All of the drinks go well with the oysters, salads, burgers, and sandwiches. Chef Chris DeBarr is always tinkering

Chris McMillian is a cocktail historian extraordinaire. His depth of knowledge, his stories, and his unassuming charm make him one of the best bartenders in the country. You will learn something new with each drink.

Left: Charcuterie.

Top right: Steak and fries.

Bottom right: The welcoming bar.

with the menu, thinking about what to add in the way of innovation grounded in tradition. One of the things that is often not a part of bar tradition is vegetables, although it is probably possible to find a few pickles on bars. Chef Chris makes a roasted vegetable plate that is outstanding. The vegetables are seasoned with pesto and balsamic vinegar and include eggplant, Vidalia onions, and bright, multicolored bell peppers.

133 N. Carrollton Ave.
New Orleans, LA
504-309-6122

TABLEAU

Pre-theater dining around the corner from Jackson Square

One of New Orleans's most historic theaters was in trouble. Le Petit Théâtre du Vieux Carré had fallen on hard times in the economic downturn of 2011, and was on the verge of permanent closure nearly a century after opening its doors in artist-filled Jackson Square. Enter Dickie Brennan stage left, whose idea to renovate the building and turn it into a restaurant alongside Le Petit Théâtre would prove to produce a brilliant synergy between the two.

Tableau, the restaurant side of this new partnership, serves patrons Louisiana Creole fare before they are whisked right next door to enjoy any of the contemporary or classic dramas, musicals, or comedies that Le Petit puts on year round. At intermission, they might step back over to the Tableau side for another bite or a drink between the acts.

There's no need to wait for curtain call to enjoy Tableau, however, since the restaurant is open even while the theater sleeps. It's the home of the bottomless mimosa and a place where even late risers can enjoy brunch every day. Eggs Benedict, steak and eggs, shrimp and grits, and veal grillades and grits are all available.

Brunch and dinner can be enjoyed indoors or out. A balcony looks over the French Quarter for sipping cocktails, eating dinner, and indulging in some people watching. This restaurant offers lots of choices. Shrimp remoulade, truffled crab claws, and oysters vol au vent are great starters. Soups and salads are also available for yet another course. These include a wedge salad, Creole French onion soup, turtle soup, and gumbo. Beef fillet, chicken, lamb chops, and more are all available and steeped in tradition. These dishes can be made even more delightful by adding shrimp, crabmeat, or even artichokes over the top. Desserts such as lemon meringue mousse, dark chocolate cake, and various ice creams and sorbets are available. It's worth noting

Top: French onion soup.

Left: Seafood sampler.

that Tableau offers a special pre-theater menu on show nights, so that guests won't miss that opening number next door.

The bar has a good selection of original cocktails, knowledgeable bartenders who can make classic cocktails, and an excellent wine selection. Tableau is a good choice for conversation. It has a lovely atmosphere, and the noise level is quite under control. They manage to make the fact that they are in the middle of the French Quarter an asset for diners, placing them on balconies and letting them enjoy the quirkiness of Jackson Square.

616 St. Peter St.
New Orleans, LA
504-934-3463
tableaufrenchquarter.com

DOOKY CHASE'S RESTAURANT

A classic restaurant presided over by the Queen of Creole cuisine

A trip to New Orleans absolutely requires a meal at Dooky Chase's Restaurant. It's a family affair. Started by Dooky Chase and his wife, Emily, in 1939, the place started as a bar and sandwich shop. It became a restaurant in 1941. Early on, the bar and restaurant established itself as a cultural mainstay for the city's African American population. In part, it served the practical purpose of cashing black workers' paychecks on Friday nights, since there were few black-owned banks. Later, especially during the 1960s, it would serve as a strategic meeting place for committed advocates of the Civil Rights movement, even hosting Dr. Martin Luther King Jr.

Dooky Chase Jr. and his wife, Leah, transformed the place into an iconic restaurant serving food that represents the traditional Creole canon. Chef Leah, known as the Queen of Creole Cuisine, serves up the best fried chicken, shrimp and white beans, and other traditional New Orleans favorites. Additionally, they built up a formidable collection of African American art that would serve as one of the city's first galleries for black artists. For her contributions to the art

> The art on the walls of Dooky Chase is truly outstanding. It is a major collection of African American art by such artists as Elizabeth Catlett, John Scott, and David Driskell, among many others. The restaurant intentionally cultivated and created opportunities for African American artists when there were few institutional opportunities for collecting their work or displaying it.

The exterior.

world, Mrs. Chase is an honorary lifetime trustee of the New Orleans Museum of Fine Arts.

Today Dooky Chase is open for lunch from Tuesday through Friday and for dinner on Friday. Look for red beans and rice, stuffed shrimp, and shrimp Clemenceau. The fried chicken was named Best Fried Chicken in New Orleans by nola.com. It is so good that instead of dessert, people have been known to order a piece of fried chicken.

Chef Leah, now a nonagenarian, can still be found in her restaurant every day that the restaurant is open. She has written cookbooks, appeared on cooking shows, and mentored more chefs than can be counted. But be sure to call before you decide to visit, because the restaurant is not open every day and almost never in the evening. It is worth the trip for the real taste of New Orleans. Mrs. Chase has fed presidents, civil rights leaders, and just plain hungry folks. If you get the buffet, you can taste a bit of all of the dishes. You can be sure to leave sated, and knowing more about the taste of New Orleans than you knew before you sat down.

2301 Orleans Ave.
New Orleans, LA
504-821-0600
dookychaserestaurant.com

ANTOINE'S

Feeding New Orleans since 1840

You really cannot miss eating at Antoine's if you're in New Orleans. It is the oldest continuously operating restaurant, operated by the original family, in the United States. It was founded in 1840 as a boarding house that served food. Soon, their food was more important than the rest of their business, and it became a restaurant. Being in Antoine's is like being in a museum. The place evokes the nineteenth century without even trying. The food has changed as the years have passed, but it is still a touchstone of the past. The shrimp remoulade, oysters Foch, souflée potatoes, oysters Rockefeller, and café brûlot diabolique are waiting for you. Antoine's has influenced the food of New Orleans and the entire country through the years. Today, restaurants still serve oysters Rockefeller, arguing over whether there is spinach or absinthe in the recipe. The family refuses to resolve the much-debated question, leaving the secret of the recipe a tantalizing mystery.

The weekday lunch at Antoine's is priced according to the current year, so in 2019 it is $20.19. It's not only a bargain, it's way to eat history. And while you are there, you should take the opportunity to walk through the entire restaurant. Antoine's is a very large restaurant with many private rooms. There are rooms dedicated to the various Mardi Gras krewes, with photos and artifacts reflecting the history of

There is no place like Antoine's. The Rex Room, with photos of former kings of carnival, old invitations framed and matted, and other memorabilia of Mardi Gras, is a mandatory stop on your visit. Each year, all of the old krewes have a meal at Antoine's and raise a glass to the past and the future. No matter what is happening, it is always at Antoine's, the restaurant that grounds the traditions of the city.

Left: Dungeon room.

Right: Antoine's Classics from its 175th anniversary menu.

the meals eaten there. The krewes actually use those rooms and have dedicated the rooms with photos and memorabilia.

The wait staff at Antoine's are professionals in the old sense of the word. They have special relationships with their customers, remembering their drinks and favorite dishes, and taking care of them on a personal level. Even if you do not have a special server, if you ask their name, how long they've has worked at Antoine's and other pertinent questions, you will be treated to a real experience that has been passed down for generations.

The food at Antoine's is full of fresh seafood. The kitchen perfected frying, and will embellish fish with lump crabmeat or shrimp. The souflée potatoes are a light and delicious appetizer. The side dishes are classic. The shrimp Creole is still prepared in the classic way. Eating in this traditional restaurant is at once a modern and historical experience. Yes, it is about the food, but it's also about the history.

Antoine's has a very good and extensive wine list, with some wines available by the glass. A glass of wine, soufflée potatoes, and the signature dessert of baked Alaska would be a wonderful snack.

If you don't have time for a meal, drink a Sazerac at the Hermes Bar at Antoine's for a glimpse, if not a taste, of the history within.

713 St. Louis St.
New Orleans, LA
504-581-4422
antoines.com

K-PAUL'S LOUISIANA KITCHEN

Innovative Cajun food with deep roots in New Orleans

Paul Prudhomme was a special man in New Orleans during his life. The culmination of his contributions might be establishing his restaurant in the French Quarter in 1979, which he opened after leaving Commander's Palace. As a Cajun with Creole training, he became the de facto interpreter of these two iconic cuisines for the rest of America through his restaurant, cookbooks, and PBS television series, *Always Cooking!*

Chef Paul continued to be a hero in the post–Hurricane Katrina era. He was quick to open his international spice factory, Magic Seasonings Company, by renting trailers for his employees—which he lined up in the parking lot—to make sure that his employees could continue to earn money. He also used proceeds from the spice business to keep the

Chef Paul Prudhomme invented blackened redfish. Seen by the general public as a traditional Cajun treatment of redfish, Prudhomme found himself at the center of a controversy. Blackened redfish as cooked by Chef Paul was highly seasoned, but not overly spicy. It became interpreted as a treatment that meant mouth-searing hot. In turn, that treatment became so popular that redfish were over fished to the point of threatening them with extinction. It became necessary to restrict fishing to help the fish re-establish themselves. That encouraged chefs to apply the technique to other ingredients, demonstrating the power of food to change the world.

Gumbo.

French Quarter restaurant open until tourists returned. He spoke up as a vocal ambassador and advocate on behalf of the city.

In the early days of the restaurant, before the renovation that expanded seating, there were lines down the street and seating was communal. Today, the wonderful and innovative cuisine is still served, but diners do not have to wait for a seat, and they don't have to share tables. It serves Chef Paul's special interpretation of Cajun and Creole food in a casual atmosphere. His stuffed eggplant (sunken eggplant pirogue), his gumbo, anything served blackened in K-Paul's, and his fried oysters served with almost anything, are all great choices.

Chef Paul has taught many chefs in New Orleans, specifically imparting the skill of layering flavors. He was a great and generous mentor, and local chefs who worked with him continue to sing his praises. Those lessons can be tasted at K-Paul's. Because of his accomplished palate, he was able to amass a large wine list that works with the highly seasoned, but not too spicy, food that is served at the restaurant. So wine drinkers will be happy. And, of course, beer and cocktails are also available to balance out all that Cajun and Creole flavor.

416 Chartres St.
New Orleans, LA
504-596-2530
kpauls.com

TODAY'S KETCH SEAFOOD

The freshest seafood around

One reason the people of New Orleans eat so much seafood is that there is such fresh and delicious seafood just hours from their tables. And because the seafood is so abundant, it's not as expensive. New Orleans has also historically been a Roman Catholic city, and because of that it was a place where meat was not eaten on Fridays. This is no longer an all-year requirement of the Catholic Church, although many Catholics still abstain from eating meat on Fridays during Lent. It's a local joke that the sacrifice of not eating meat is hardly a sacrifice at all. It is something accepted without reluctance in favor of eating shrimp, crab, oysters, and other interesting fish. With all this seafood consumption, freshness is at a premium. Asking people to eat seafood that is not well prepared or that isn't fresh is really unacceptable.

At Today's Ketch, there is always fresh seafood being sold and served, sometimes the very same day that it's caught. This isn't exotic fish like salmon or lobster; this fish is hyper local. Here you can get po'boys of fried seafood served on fresh bread. This means fried shrimp, fried oysters, fried fish, and fried soft shell crabs. The seafood could not be fresher, and the frying is done with a light touch. Nothing is overcooked, it's wonderful. Teri Pohlman, who owns the place with her husband, Jeff, prepares the food and has developed the recipes. All of her seasonings and other recipes are top secret. They have been preparing, serving, and selling fresh, fresh seafood since 1985.

If you don't want a po'boy, these same fried delicacies are available as a seafood plate, which comes with a salad and two sides. The sides

The prepared foods like gumbo, stuffed artichokes, shrimp salad, and other simple prepared foods are made fresh every day. This place is a gem that is only known by locals. It is an authentic experience of good eating with no frills.

Left: A mess of crabs.
Right: Fresh fish for sale.

include a baked potato, fried potatoes, macaroni and cheese, sweet potato fries, or a really good medley of fresh vegetables. And there is shrimp salad, gumbo, and so much more. One of the best features of the restaurant is its simplicity. It serves boiled crabs, boiled shrimp, and boiled crawfish, which is served piled on trays on the table. It is up to you to peel and eat your pile of goodness.

What is remarkable about Today's Ketch is that it is also a seafood market. Freshly shucked oysters, raw soft-shell crabs, shrimp sorted into different sizes, and filets of various types of fish are being sold in the same place where people are eating. There is the wafting smell of the cooking food, but there is never the slightest fishy smell. People are casually dressed and pleasantly eating. It's a friendly place with lots of regulars who tease each other. Besides the fresh seafood, there are frozen offerings for sale, like alligator meat, frog legs, and frozen soft-shell crabs.

This place is an experience. It's a way to see what the seafood choices are like in the New Orleans area. There is no cream sauce, cheese, almonds, or nuts to blunt the taste of the food. It's worth the trip to St. Bernard to eat unassuming seafood that is absolutely delicious.

2110 Judge Perez Dr.
Chalmette, LA
504-279-6639
todaysketch.com

HERBSAINT BAR AND RESTAURANT

Donald Link's flagship restaurant on St. Charles Avenue

If there's an accolade left for Herbsaint to win for its French-Southern cuisine with rustic Italian elements, you'd be hard-pressed to identify it. Just a smattering of its many trophies include being named one of *Gourmet* magazine's 50 Best Restaurants in America, one of Eater National's Best Restaurants in America, and securing a coveted spot on the *Times-Picayune*'s 10 Best New Orleans Restaurants every single year since they started publishing the list. More personally, this was the restaurant that propelled founding chef Donald Link to win the James Beard Foundation award for Best Chef South in 2007. Imagine his pride when the restaurant's current chef, Rebecca Wilcomb, won the very same award in 2017.

All of these honors (and more) are well deserved—this is a delightful place to eat. Link describes his restaurant as a contemporary take on a French bistro, but there is no denying the slightly Italian bent of some of the dishes and the clearly Cajun influences in the use of Andouille, boudin, and tasso. This is clearly the place where new ideas in food can be explored by Donald Link.

Herbsaint proudly lets you know who supplies them with their delicious ingredients. If this is important to you, you can check out the Herbsaint website to see not only who these suppliers are, but also where they are located. The restaurant is open for lunch and dinner every day. You can always find gumbo, there's a changing soup special, and the watermelon gazpacho served with lump crabmeat is especially delicious and refreshing during the hot months.

Small plates are intensely flavored delights. The joy of the small plates is that after eating one and going to another, there is a delightful series

Left: Gnocchi.
Right: On St. Charles Avenue.

of flavor explosions. For example, baked Asiago with lemon and oregano is a great beginning. There's a fried oyster plate, gnocchi with pancetta, and Sicilian beef with anchovies. Every day there is a new vegetable selection plus fries and dirty rice. The bacon and fried oyster sandwich is one of the best sandwiches ever.

For the main course there are a number of choices. The fish of the day is always available and could be anything from a fin fish to soft shell crabs. There's a tuna sandwich; crispy goat with cauliflower, black beans, and yogurt; duck leg confit with dirty rice; and also a lamb dish, a shrimp dish, and steak with fries.

And then there is dessert. These are more than marvelous. Be forewarned that it is imperative that you leave room for dessert. Coconut custard pie served with buttermilk Chantilly and orange caramel is really not to be missed. There's also a malted milk chocolate mousse and fried blueberry pie with Creole cream cheese ice cream. There are various flavors of ice cream, and at night a cheese plate is available.

The food is quite varied, but the extensive wine list is more than adequate in balancing out the flavors of the table. The beer list is equally impressive, and the cocktail program is also very good. The house specialties are all interesting, and the bartenders are old hands at making traditional cocktails.

701 St. Charles Ave.
New Orleans, LA
504-524-4114
herbsaint.com

BROUSSARD'S

Classic French dishes in the French Quarter

In the days when founding chef Joseph Broussard reigned, the lights of the restaurant were dimmed for the serving of Napoleon brandy in honor of the general, while the wait staff would sing a round of "La Marseillaise." Broussard's Francophilia began during his own training in France, before he moved into the Borello Masion and founded the restaurant there with his wife in 1920. That fascination is still reflected in the bee decor found throughout the restaurant as an homage to Napoleon Bonaparte himself.

In 2013 the Ammari family began its role as keepers of the Broussard's flame, and today Executive Chef Gy Reinbolt prepares classic French dishes with a Creole flair. Broussard's opened in its historic Vieux Carré location with local Creole food and products, showcasing traditional French dishes. Today the restaurant continues the tradition with a refined blend of French and Creole influences.

The menu includes chilled asparagus soup, goat cheese tart, and Broussard's Caesar. Traditional main entrées are given a Creole twist: sous-vide chicken Provençal, summer vegetable bouillabaisse, moules frites, and cane-glazed pork tenderloin. For dessert you can find emperor's fool (blueberries, Chantilly cream, honey, and almond tuille), vanilla bean crème brûlée, and mousse au chocolat. Broussard's has both a prix fixe menu and a full à la carte menu. Guests can choose from starters, soups, salads, a broad range of fresh Gulf seafood selections, and half a dozen meat and poultry dishes.

Now approaching its centennial anniversary, Broussard's has a robust wine list featuring affordable bottles. It has received recognition for many years from *Wine Spectator* magazine. During happy hour, guests will find discounted featured cocktails and a selection of reasonably priced menu items. Choose the crab and corn beignets, shrimp

Top left: The dining room. Credit: J Stephen Young.

Bottom left: The courtyard. Credit: J Stephen Young.

Right: Lump crab ravigote salad.

remoulade, or crabmeat ravigote as snacks in the bar. If you are in the mood for a meat snack, try a Cajun slider—beef and smoked cheese on brioche.

Broussard's is open for dinner every night and for brunch on Friday through Monday. The courtyard at Broussard's provides one of the most beautiful settings for a delicious meal or a drink. When the weather is right, this is a perfect choice for outdoor dining. And the staff is very good about extending service to the courtyard so that you are attended as well as in any indoor space.

819 Conti St.
New Orleans, LA
504-581-3866
broussards.com

ANGELO BROCATO ORIGINAL ITALIAN ICE CREAM PARLOR

An old Sicilian gelateria and pasticeria

The Sicilians of New Orleans have a practice of thanking St. Joseph for his intercession on their behalf. They thank him by creating a St. Joseph altar on St. Joseph Day, March 19th. Altars can be in someone's home or in a church community center, a restaurant, or even a bar or a grocery store. The cookies that are made by Angelo Brocato's Bakery can be found on these altars all over the city. The cookies include sesame seed cookies, anise-flavored iced cookies, and fried dough formed in the shape of pine cones. These cookies can be bought at Brocato's, at groceries in the area, and are regularly found on altars during the St. Joseph Day celebrations.

Many people remember the act of faith that the re-opening of Brocato's after Hurricane Katrina represented. In 2005 the family embarked on an ambitious renovation in time to celebrate the 100th anniversary of the opening of the first Brocato store at its original location. That was July, and the very next month Hurricane Katrina flooded the city and devastated the work that had just been completed. With the support of the people of New Orleans—who felt that the city couldn't go on without Brocato's—the restaurant opened before the neighborhood had really come back. So people flocked there, patiently waiting in line to buy traditional gelato or granita, for a taste of nostalgia, and to be reminded how resilient the city really is. It was a touchstone to taste memory. You can visit and taste that, too.

This very old New Orleans ice cream parlor served an old-style gelato before gelato was cool. It was founded over one hundred years ago by Angelo Brocato himself, who brought generations of gelato

Left: St. Joseph altar.
Right: Cannoli.

wisdom with him from Palermo, Sicily, where he was raised and apprenticed. The gelato on offer is traditional in its flavors, such as spumoni, pistachio, torroncino, and stracciatella. Brocato's also offers traditional Sicilian granita, such as a lemon ice. Another delicious choice is the watermelon ice. It's such fresh watermelon, in fact, that you'll sometimes come across the occasional watermelon seed included in the dish or package. Other ices include peach, blood orange, strawberry, blackberry, and cantaloupe, depending on the season.

Besides the frozen delights, Brocato's serves other house-made desserts such as cannoli and all manner of biscotti. Cakes, meringues, and dishes of biscotti can be ordered in the restaurant. You can also order a whole cake or large quantities of biscotti. Many of the pastries can be ordered in miniature sizes for single bites at parties. When you think Italian pastry, this is where you can find it—tiramisu, cassata cake, Napoleons, éclairs, ricotta pie—and strudel, Greek pastries, and fruit tarts. There are wonderful restaurants in the neighborhood around Brocato's. But even if the desserts at those places are wonderful, many people will leave the restaurant in favor of a short walk to Angelo Brocato's for a bowl of gelato or a slice of something delightful and traditional.

214 N. Carrollton Ave.
New Orleans, LA
504-486-0078
angelobrocatoicecream.com

MOSQUITO SUPPER CLUB

Bringing the bounty of the waters of Louisiana

Melissa Martin knows that the stories of the bayou are best told with no rush, over good food made by the people who know it best. Her tables at the Mosquito Supper Club aren't large, but they'll always be full, and so will your stomach and heart after visiting this Cajun treasure. Here, food is more than just nourishment, it's part of the narrative itself, and it's worth being part of the story.

If you can plan just a little, try to reserve a place at the Mosquito Supper Club. This will be your opportunity to experience genuine Cajun home cooking, prepared by an experienced and passionate chef. Meals are served family style, with groups around several large tables. You must make reservations because each dinner service is limited to one seating of twenty-four people, Thursday through Sunday.

The menu is entirely seasonal, so you cannot know what will be served, nor are substitutions available. You can be assured, however, that whatever arrives at your place will be delicious and surprising. A sample evening enjoyed at the Mosquito Supper Club might begin

Mosquito Supper Club is located on one side of a shotgun double on Dryades Street. The other side is occupied by Seasoned. This wonderful shop is full of vintage cookware, serving pieces, and appliances. Whether you see things that remind you of your grandmother's kitchen—that you had to have—or that gently used copper pot that is now affordable, a trip to Seasoned is always fun. It's the place to find the perfect baby shower or wedding gift that you can be sure no one else will be giving. They have best tea towels and napkins, the most interesting salt-and-pepper shakers, and the most delightful vintage baby bibs. Go prepared to indulge yourself—it is irresistible.

Peeling crawfish.

with the cucumber and tomato salad—kissed with the lightest of dressings to enhance the natural flavors of the fruits. The crab toast is sautéed lightly in butter and served on tasty bread made by Levee Bakery. (Levee Bakery is a bakery owned by Christina Balzebrea, who holds a pop-up bakery sale at the site every Saturday.) The parsley and other herbs are fresh. The shrimp and okra still smell of the bayou and the field. The fish is the freshest possible. The desserts are fresh fruits, pies, and ice cream that make the meal complete.

Chef Melissa Martin, born in Chauvin, Louisiana, is the spirit behind this eatery. The family style makes you feel like you are her guests for dinner. The food is scrupulously fresh and prepared with great respect for the ingredients and traditions of the bayou Cajuns. You can rely on the food being incredibly good and surprising. She is proud of her Cajun roots and its traditions and committed to practicing sustainability in order to protect the fast-diminishing coastline of Louisiana. Her entire extended family is involved with provisioning the restaurant. And that rootedness is what she wants to present. It's also what makes this restaurant so very special.

This is a BYOB dinner. So with foresight—make a reservation, buy and bring a bottle or two—you will have an extraordinary experience. Not only is the food outstanding, but by sitting at long tables family style with like-minded diners, you may make new friends. You'll also gain a wonderful new appreciation for the goodness of eating with others, sharing stories and food.

3824 Dryades St.
New Orleans, LA
504-517-0374
mosquitosupperclub.com

TUJAGUE'S RESTAURANT

The second-oldest restaurant in New Orleans, and it's still fresh

One of the oldest restaurants in the city, Tujague's is a special place to eat both because it's an example of the past, present, and future of the city's historic restaurants. Unlike Antoine's, the city's other really old restaurant, Tujague's has been owned by many different proprietors beginning with the family it is named after. At its inception, Tujague's had no menu. It was a bistro in the oldest sense of the word. It was only a generation ago that the menu was fixed so there was no need to write it down. Daily there was a boiled brisket with horseradish sauce, maybe chicken bonne femme, or maybe fish. You merely made a choice of fish, beef, or chicken. What do you expect from a restaurant that opened in 1856?

In 1914 Tujague's moved from its original location on Decatur Street into the restaurant just a few buildings down and took over the corner. That restaurant had belonged to their stiffest competition, Madame Begue. Today the Latter family owns the restaurant, but it has been meticulous in honoring the bistro's honored traditions. And it now has a printed menu. That menu still contains the beef brisket and the remoulade-covered boiled shrimp that drove many people to eat there. And coffee can still be found served in glasses instead of cups. Presidents, writers, actors, and other celebrities have eaten at Tujague's over the years.

When you visit, remember its traditions and order the shrimp remoulade and the beef brisket. But when you return, you can explore the menu a bit more by trying the gumbo and turtle soup, the various oyster and shrimp dishes, the duck, drum, trout, veal, and pork chops. Tujague's is still a neighborhood restaurant in the sense that people hang out there regularly and know the staff and one another. That is

Left: Grasshopper.
Right: Crawfish and goat cheese crepes.

a treat to see. It's an example of restaurants and bars being places of gathering and not just a place to drink or eat. It's even the kind of place where you might learn the news of the neighborhood.

Be sure to spend a moment appreciating the bar, which is approaching its second century. This bar survived Prohibition, various wars, and seems to have absorbed the memories of all who have stood there for a drink. It would be a fine place for a Sazerac. The period of Prohibition had the bar serving lemonade and iced tea at the bar, but serving drinks on the sly in the room right behind the bar. When Prohibition ended, the bartenders applied themselves in entering cocktail contests and inventing cocktails. The drink that survives even today is the grasshopper. Tujague's claims to have invented this cream and crème de menthe, light-green dessert drink. If you are there, that is what you should try for dessert. Drinking one in the place where it was invented is part of the experience.

823 Decatur St.
New Orleans, LA
504-525-8676
tujaguesrestaurant.com

PYTHIAN MARKET

A traditional food hall in the city center

Now a food hall, Pythian Market is located in a building dripping with history. The Pythian was the home of the Colored Knights of Pythias. Built in 1908, the building was a dominant feature in the neighborhood, and it played a key role in the early movement for African American civil rights as a center of African American culture. The building was bustling with a theater and businesses, and it even had a garden on the roof where jazz could be heard. The Pythian building is a mixture of residential, commercial, and market use.

The Pythian considers itself a food collective. It has a really interesting mixture of food stalls in the hall, which makes it possible for you to visit some of the city's specialties all in one place. You'll find microversions of many of the most highly reviewed restaurants (some of them in this very book!), all ready for you to sample their fare. For example, there is a strong Vietnamese influence that has changed the food of the city. It's possible to eat at a Vietnamese restaurant or one that is just influenced by the Vietnamese palate. You can find such an eatery in Eatwell at the Pythian. At Fete au Fete you can experience more traditional food of Louisiana, both Cajun and Creole dishes.

Kais is a seafood house that is greatly influenced by Asian flavors and techniques. It serves lots of vegetables and poke, as well as sushi, all with interesting combinations of different flavors of Asia. 1908, the bar named for date that the Pythian opened, is a wine bar with a serious beer collection and cocktails crafted like food. Central City BBQ is an offshoot of the barbecue restaurant located in Central City near the Dryades Public Market. Imagine your trip to the Pythian Market where you could get a glass of wine, some barbecue, a bit of sushi or poke, or Cajun food. And that's not all.

Meribo is a pizza place. The Middle East is represented—hummus, yogurt, and vegetables—at Little Fig, a smaller version of 1000 Figs,

Left: Poulet chicken wrap. Credit: Randy P. Schmidt.
Right: Little Fig hummus plate. Credit: Randy P. Schmidt.

the well established restaurant on Esplanade Avenue. Roustabout Coffee Company is the coffee representative at the Pythian Market, so that all through the day you can get a good cup of coffee or espresso to keep you moving. La Cocinita is a restaurant with a blend of Latin American street flavors. The food truck, La Cocinita, can be found parked around the city.

The Pythian Market is a fun amalgam of many restaurants. There are many options that are vegetarian, and some vegan. There's so much variety, in fact, it is hard to imagine that anyone could be unsuccessful in finding something to satisfy them. The lovely space gives you options to eat in the hall or to take your food away. One option is to go to Duncan Plaza across the street from the Pythian to eat outside. Another option is to return to your room or an office and enjoy your meal. Or depending on the time, perhaps taking your food to your room for a quiet evening watching movies on TV is an option.

234 Loyola Ave.
New Orleans, LA
504-481-9599
pythianmarket.com

HEARD DAT KITCHEN

A take-out food stop with fine-dining food

This neighborhood gem is located in Central City and run by chef/
owner Jeffery Heard. You'll recognize it by the huge red crawfish
that beckons from the exterior wall. Heard knows what he's doing
in the kitchen, after having worked under Chef John Besh's tutelage
and at the W Hotel. He has serious traditional food values. He
opened his place with the determination to make really great food
for an affordable price in his own neighborhood. And he works right
alongside his family—his wife and children. Chef Heard explains that
he may have polished his skills in restaurants, but he learned to cook
from his mother. That's probably why he named the catering wing of
the business after her, Audrey Mae.

Chef Heard can produce a mean ya-ka mein, the wonderful noodle
dish that is New Orleans's own version of pho or ramen, also known as
Old Sober. It's prepared with chunks of meat and a rich broth. If you've
been away from New Orleans, it's one of those unique dishes—found
nowhere else—that let you know you're actually home. And he does
make a mean fried chicken po'boy.

You can eat here in the few spaces inside and out that can
accommodate seating. Eating inside lets you watch the people who
know a good New Orleans meal when they find one. Most people
stop in for take out, however, earning Heard Dat its fame for being
"gourmet to go." The dishes are all unquestionably New Orleans, but
these are also very personal dishes. You can find lobster and corn and
cream together. The whimsy of the dishes' names reflect the chef's
creativity. The Dat Superdome is a huge dish that includes a filet of fish
covered with mashed potatoes, hence the reference to the Superdome.

All of the creamy dishes are redolent of black pepper. There is
nothing bland and nothing simple about the taste of any of the dishes
on the menu. And there's nothing skimpy about any of the portions,
either. Be prepared for very rich dishes and not much offered for those

Top: Shrimp over pasta.

Bottom left: All the fried goodness.

Bottom right: Salmon and asparagus.

looking for light fare. If that's what you want, go somewhere else. It's also not a place to go for sweets. The only dessert is the classic bread pudding. But if you want New Orleans, you will get it here.

2520 Felicity St.
New Orleans, LA
504-510-4248

CAFÉ CONTI

Breakfast and lunch right in the heart of the French Quarter

Guests lucky enough to be waking up in the Prince Conti Hotel in the middle of the French Quarter don't have far to go for a healthy breakfast—the Café Conti is inside the building. There they can fill up on hearty and delicious fare before hitting all the sights within walking distance. Luckily for everyone else, the restaurant isn't just for hotel guests—or any of the ghosts rumored to linger in the historic building—and everyone can take advantage of this charming café. Let one of the daily specials listed outside on a traditional chalkboard be your guide.

Crepes are the basis for the menu at Café Conti. Owners David Smith and Doug Hary wanted to create a place to eat lighter food as a break for travelers who have overdosed on exotic New Orleans fare. The savory crepes include very creative combinations like crab and Brie or bacon and Gruyère crepes. The creamed spinach, egg, bacon, and Gruyère crepe is like a quiche crepe—surprising and delicious. Chicken, mushroom, and cheese crepes are a good choice. And there is a vegetable and cheese choice for those who want a vegetarian option.

The Nutella and banana sweet crepe makes a wonderful dessert or a decadent breakfast. Although any of the sweet crepes would taste delicious with a cup of coffee for breakfast, the chocolate and strawberry crepe is a real treat. Mixed berries with crème Anglaise is a delight.

Omelets are very good, accompanied by grits or potatoes. And then the choices are up to you. Various kinds of cheese, sausage, mushrooms, tomatoes, peppers, and ham will fill up your omelet and your belly to start the day. Every day there is a variation of eggs Benedict. You just

Put an egg on your rustic spinach crepe.

have to wait until you're there to know what is on offer. The European is a baguette with Brie and ham with sliced tomato. Eating a European seems very appropriate in the setting and in the French Quarter. The breakfast po'boy—po'boy bread with scrambled eggs, smoked sausage, cheese, and tomato—is a fun play on the classic po'boy. Why not give it a try? And there is a lox and bagel combination.

A shrimp and grits choice works for either breakfast or lunch. The grits bowl is a clever riff on a noodle bowl with egg, bacon, and creamed spinach. There are salad choices, which help you build a balanced meal. And the "sides" that are available can help create a creative omelet, salad, or crepe.

830 Conti St.
New Orleans, LA
504-636-1060
cafeconti.com

ATOMIC BURGER

Milkshakes fit for the Jetsons

While brothers Nick and Joe Spitale understand that making burgers and shakes is still making fast food, they just want to make sure it's also *good* food. They founded Atomic Burger in 2013 on Veterans Highway in Metairie, a suburb that blends seamlessly into New Orleans.

To set their restaurant apart, they decided to elevate their burgers and set high standards by grinding their own meat, using real potatoes for the hand-cut fries, and making shakes with real ingredients instead of powdered mixes. And the critics agree—*Thrillist* magazine even named its burger one of the Top 100 in America.

Biting into one of those burgers, your mouth feels transported back in time to those classic diners, but the atmosphere of Atomic Burger is modern and even futuristic. To satisfy those with more modern—or restrained—palates, a turkey burger and a portobello mushroom burger fit the bill. A bright and airy "Jetsons"-style decor provides the perfect backdrop for one of the most futuristic menu items: milkshakes chilled by liquid nitrogen! The flavors here include some interesting choices, like Nutella-marshmallow and salted caramel. There are also, of course, the traditional chocolate, vanilla, and strawberry.

This restaurant is family friendly, with either a slider or a hot dog available for children and those with a smaller appetite. The sides

> The Atomic Freeze milkshake is delicious, but the fact that they use liquid nitrogen to cool it is just plain fun. Salted caramel, peanut butter-chocolate chip, and blueberry cheesecake flavors are just plain fun, too.

Top: Atomic Burger interior.
Left: Atomic Burger classics.

include hand-cut fries with one of the special sauces they make. There is another side option, probably more Jetsons than 1950s diner: steamed edamame.

3934 Veterans Blvd.
Metairie, LA
504-309-7474
theatomicburger.com

COQUETTE

A smart, stylish restaurant with food to match

There's nothing quite like a baptism by fire to forge a kitchen novice into a master chef. This experience came early for Maryland Eastern Shore native, Chef Michael Stoltzfus, when his mother unexpectedly opened a bakery and employed teenage Michael as a short-order breakfast and lunch cook. He may not have seen this turn in the road coming, but it's definitely led him down a path to success. He catapulted up the ranks of culinary development and opened Coquette in December of 2008.

If you are looking for a place where the food is special, the location casual, and the price point sweet, try a meal at Coquette. The food is very future forward, but feels satisfying and comforting at the same time. Somehow, they have found the sweet spot that bridges tradition with modernity. Chef Kristen Essig joined the team in 2016, and the two have built up the restaurant in a late nineteenth century building in Uptown New Orleans. During different eras, the building has served as a residence, grocery store, and even an auto parts store. The renovation of the building is very modern, but manages to allow for cozy areas with a traditional feel. The restaurant is definitely good enough for a special occasion, but also makes for a great neighborhood spot.

Coquette is open on Mondays and closed on Tuesdays. That is important to know in the city, because Monday is the traditional dark day in New Orleans. When you are at a loss for where to eat on a Monday, Coquette is likely the place. But don't forget that on Tuesdays, you will have to eat somewhere else. What should you eat there? The tasting menu is perfect for a celebration. You just entrust yourself to the judgment of the chef. And not knowing what is to come is part of the experience. Or try the fried chicken. It is so good. Try the eggplant au poivre with chanterelles, crab, and nectarines. This eggplant and crab on the plate is a wonder.

Top: Fried chicken.
Right: Mike and Kristen.

Chef Stoltzfus has been nominated as a semi-finalist for the "Best Chef in the South" by the James Beard Foundation, been recognized by *Food & Wine* magazine and *New Orleans* magazine, and yet he still cooks. That is one of the really important aspects of Coquette. The chefs still cook there as opposed to directing cooks from off-site. Their presence at Coquette is noted, especially as it helps them create daily specials with the best that the farm and market have to offer.

2800 Magazine St.
New Orleans, LA
504-265-0421
coquettenola.com

GALATOIRE'S

The most fun bistro in the city

As one of the old-line restaurants in New Orleans, Galatoire's holds a very important place in the heart of the city. But it's not some stuffy, hidebound old place. Galatoire's is the jokester of the old-line restaurants. It's the place where waiters and the entire restaurant will sing Happy Birthday to you. It's the place where on Fridays, regulars start by eating lunch and stay right on through dinner. This is the place where people table hop throughout the restaurant, where people are dressed up to eat, and where they spontaneously socialize with people at the tables around them.

The restaurant was founded in 1905 by Jean Galatoire, who was born in Pardies, France. Jean purchased a well-known mid-nineteenth-century restaurant, Victor's, and made it his own. The restaurant still has involvement from the fourth generation of the Galatoire family. The food is traditional New Orleans food served in a French bistro manner with a few traditional French homey dishes still available. It is definitely a place that still values professional wait staff. And if you know someone who eats at Galatoire's often, ask for a server recommendation.

The menu at Galatoire's has been modernized without taking away the traditional simplicity of the food. Trout amandine or meunière are standards. The kitchen can apply these styles to any fish or soft-shell crab. It's common to ask your waiter to add lump crabmeat to your grilled fish. The menu is heavy with seafood—shrimp, oysters, crabmeat, and often crawfish. The Galatoire Goute—or taste of Galatoire—allows seafood lovers to taste three different boiled seafood salads: crab maison, crawfish maison, and shrimp remoulade. Your server may be able to embellish that plate with oysters en brochette to complete your seafood medley. The salads reflect the seafood-heavy style of the restaurant. While eating appetizers and starters can make it hard to leave room for the main courses, lamb chops, veal, and traditional chicken dishes are the stars here.

Oysters.

The turtle soup is laced with sherry, the okra and seafood gumbo is always tempting, and the darker-rouxed duck and Andouille gumbo can make a satisfying first course. The Godchaux salad comes in two sizes—an appetizer size and a main dish size. It's basically an abundance of boiled shrimp and crabmeat in a lettuce salad with Creole mustard house vinaigrette. The crabmeat-stuffed avocado is another classic New Orleans salad. The iceberg wedge is drenched in blue cheese dressing. The salad with hearts of palm and asparagus is a wonderful starter.

Chicken Clemenceau is a half chicken served with mushrooms and Brabant potatoes. The chicken bonne-femme is served with bacon and caramelized onions. Both of these dishes are classic New Orleans choices. The Bouillabaisse is rich with shellfish, saffron, and fish. The shrimp and crab dishes are just wonderful, and anyone would be happy with a choice made by just pointing a finger at the menu with their eyes closed.

The fish options can be grilled or served as a meunière or amandine. You can ask your server for advice depending on what is available. Galatoire's is one of the few restaurants that serves liver as a choice, along with lamb chops, veal, filets, and ribeye prepared to your specifications.

Galatoire's has a battery of professional wait staff. Regulars have a preferred server who knows what they like and can have a drink on the table before a diner is seated. When you eat here, put yourself into the server's hands. You will not be sorry.

209 Bourbon St.
New Orleans, LA
504-525-2021
galatoires.com

CASA BORREGA

A touch of real Mexico in the city

There is probably no other restaurant in the city that reflects its owners' passion more than Casa Borrega, not just in the kitchen and bar, but also in the feel of the place. Hugo Montero and Linda Stone personally restored the O.C. Haley Boulevard building with their own hands. Hugo, who hails from Mexico City, is also an artist. He used his color sensibility and artistic eye to decorate the interior, allowing his background and talent to create the authentic feel of Mexico in New Orleans.

The food presented in this lovely setting is perfect for both its taste and for the experience and ambiance. All the while, Hugo will regale you with stories while you eat, ponder the menu, or drink from his great assortment of Mexican liquor.

The menu includes tacos, tostadas, tortas, and ensaladas, as you might expect. This is not a Tex-Mex haven, but rather a true Mexican experience. The guacamole, meats, and sopas are all based on the Mexican palate. There are a few examples of cultural fusion, however, like the torta, a Mexican po'boy, that's a perfect melding of New Orleans and Mexico on your plate.

In the evening, camarones al tequila or borrego de oro will satisfy your cravings for Mexican flavors. The quesadilla de papa, served street-style, and the ceviche are both excellent examples of what to expect. And also be prepared to have at your disposal a great collection of tequilas and mezcals in the bar. Yes, there are Mexican beers, but the tequila list is amazing. You will not be disappointed.

> The best selection of tequila and mezcal can be found at the bar. If these represent your spirit of choice, you will be very happy to spend some time at Casa Borrega.

Left: A decor of Mexico.
Right: Enchiladas de pollo con mole.

This restaurant honors lamb, so don't overlook the lamb flautas and other lamb-forward dishes on the menu. Except for lamb shanks and lamb chops, there isn't a lot of lamb on the menus in New Orleans. The tres leches cake is a familiar Mexican dessert definitely worthy of a selection.

Casa Borrega serves lunch and dinner every day except Monday, when it is closed, and only brunch on Sunday. This is a place with outstanding live music and a lovely outdoor eating space. Hugo and Linda have imposed their personal sensibilities on the restaurant. You will sit in the restaurant and just smile at the colors and images that surround you.

1719 Oretha Castle Haley Blvd.
New Orleans, LA
504-427-0654
casaborrega.com

BEACHBUM BERRY'S LATITUDE 29

A tiki bar and restaurant in the French Quarter

Jeff "Beachbum" Berry, tiki author and tiki artifact collector, has combined all of his tiki skills and interests in Latitude 29. New Orleans is the perfect place for the new tiki—yes, with traditional fruity rum drinks, but also new tiki drinks from Berry's own imagination with tequila and mezcal. But in true tiki style the "Polynesian" and Creole cuisine that accompanies the drinks is also delicious and fun. The pork adobo and vegetable poke will make you happy. The drinks, including traditional communal drinks in fun tiki-style drinking vessels, are superb.

Because of his vast collection of tiki memorabilia, Berry has created a space that is uniquely decorated and endlessly interesting. The netting with starfish and other boating themes adorn the walls, just as you would expect at a proper tiki bar and restaurant. But the lamps, the screens, and the special glassware are extraordinary. The experience of being there is akin to entering a tiki museum, while still feeling modern and up-to-date. It allows you to experience the past and the present as an active participant, not just an observer. It's a real testament to Jeff Berry's generosity, his sharing of his tiki knowledge and his tiki artifacts with his customers, that's also reflected in the intelligent drinks and food.

Not only are Chef Marcel Hayes's creations imaginative and delicious, the surroundings that Berry has amassed make the experience complete. In the beachcomber style, there are small plates called dim sum, though not served dim-sum style. These include pork ribs, dumplings, and a vegetable poke. The loco moco is a huge eight-ounce patty with shitake mushrooms and a fried egg. The Caesar salad

Top: Loco moco. Credit: Sam Hanna.
Left: Banshee. Credit: Annene Kaye.

contains fried squid. Duck is served with miso grits and collard greens. A banh mi is stuffed with tofu. The Chinese chicken salad is a half-pound of chicken breast, purple cabbage, and fried wontons, dressed with the house Asian dressing. Sides include crispy green beans, collards, and shoestring fries. Do you really need a dessert with such sweet tiki drinks available? Those drinks will satisfy your sweet tooth. Mahalo.

321 N. Peters St.
New Orleans, LA
504-609-3811
latitude29nola.com

KIN

A ramen house in New Orleans

Chef Hieu Than loved the ramen places he frequented in New York City, but back home in New Orleans he realized that there were places that served ramen, but no ramen places. The distinction is an important one. After all, ramen is a simple soup. It's just starch, liquid, and protein, and yet when executed correctly, it can become the very basis for an entire restaurant concept with a cult following of its own.

Hieu Than's inspiration at Kin is excellent ramen. The noodle bowl is the centerpiece of the place. New Orleans has always had its share of noodles—with ya-ka mein a long-standing favorite and pho a standard since the 1970s. But ramen is a welcome addition to the array of noodle-bowl choices. The restaurant is a tiny jewel box where strangers can sit together to enjoy their selections. The seating is a combination of the traditional ramen style in which elevated chefs look down into the bowls of their customers and the more conventional tables and chairs. It's as wonderful as it is personal.

There is ramen every day. And specials change so that dumplings and other delicacies can find their way onto the table. There are small plates that include salads and often fermented bits. The dumplings may be filled with something surprising, like chicken Marsala. You never know what you'll find in the daily dumplings. You can definitely enjoy a meal at Kin alone, communing with other single diners, or attend the bar with a friend. Having a friend allows for sharing some of the appealing daily specials since the portions are large and incredibly satisfying. There is usually a vegan bowl that is available and definitely tasty enough to be enjoyed by anyone, vegan or not.

The broth is always rich. The noodles are house made. The vegetables gracing your bowl may not be traditional, but they are thoughtfully chosen and delicious. But it makes you remember that ramen should be made with what is available locally so that it's at its freshest. The egg

Top left: A feast in a bowl.

Top right: Noodles.

Bottom left: Chef Hieu Than.

Bottom right: Made with the greatest attention.

is always perfect. Check on the spice level before you order, because sometimes the heat is very forward. But with such a diverse selection, you'll definitely find something that you will enjoy. And have the Vietnamese iced coffee as your dessert. It will cap off your meal with just the right uplifting note.

4600 Washington Ave.
New Orleans, LA
504-304-8557
facebook.com/kinfordindin

ST. ROCH MARKET

A downtown food hall

The historic St. Roch Market—nearly destroyed by Hurricane Katrina—has been reborn as an urban food hall in the Faubourg Marigny/Bywater neighborhood. A market has served this neighborhood since the 1830s, but the current building dates to 1875, when it was one of many state-owned local markets throughout the city. These open-air markets sold every kind of food and sundry items a household might need and were stocked by independent vendors who rented stalls. As residents became more mobile and shopping patterns changed in the twentieth century, however, the private grocery store overshadowed the public markets, most of which closed.

After World War II, the St. Roch Market became Lama's Supermarket, a popular purveyor of fresh and cooked seafood. Locals could bring their own containers to the market to be filled up with Lama's delicious gumbo. In later years, various restaurants occupied the space, even as it fell into disrepair, but the final blow was Hurricane Katrina, which left only a ramshackle wooden building that was unsafe to inhabit.

Through diligent support from the city government, the building was repaired and triumphantly reopened in 2015 as a food hall housing thirteen permanent vendors who serve food and drink from New Orleans and around the world. Today the St. Roch Market seems to have found its place in the neighborhood. It's a place where you can stop in for a cup of coffee at Coast Roast Coffee or eat at a place like Fete au Fete, which offers Cajun and Creole food at the St. Roch Market as well as the Pythian Market. The Elysian Oyster Bar at St. Roch is a classic oyster bar. It offers oysters, boiled seafood in a seafood tower, gumbo, and a charcuterie and cheese combination. The Mayhaw Bar, named for the Louisiana fruit, is a place for craft cocktails, wine, and beer.

The St. Roch Market is located in Faubourg Marigny and Bywater, which is becoming a very trendy and hipster neighborhood. The

Top: From the street.

Bottom left: A variety of options.

Bottom right: A gathering place.

Market, so historic and central to the neighborhood, is an anchor in a neighborhood that is changing in the post–Hurricane Katrina New Orleans.

2381 St. Claude Ave.
New Orleans, LA
504-609-3813
neworleans.strochmarket.com

TOUPS' MEATERY

A small gem of a place near City Park

Top Chef contestant Isaac Toups's philosophy is that everyone should eat "foie gras in flip-flops." He's all about giving his customers access to incredible flavors, regardless of what they happen to look like. It's a philosophy honed over years of exploring his own Cajun heritage through its emblematic, yet ultra-casual, cuisine. And Chef Toups should know—his family has lived in this region for more than three hundred years. Now he's taken all of that heritage and distilled it into a veritable homage at Toups' Meatery.

This tiny neighborhood restaurant was opened by Chef Isaac Toups and his wife, Amanda. A true Cajun from Rayne, Louisiana, he has taken his interest in meat—from pork to beef and *everything* in between—and created a real, meat-forward restaurant. It is from here that he was plucked for television appearances and discovered to be a *Top Chef*–worthy TV personality. But anyone who eats at Toups' Meatery will also recognize that Chef Isaac is the real thing. The food served at Toups is genuinely Cajun inspired and also meaty. This is the place to eat rabbit, duck, shrimp, and crab. Those Cajun specialties like boudin balls and hog's head cheese are always available. The cornbread, cheeses, and house-cured meat board will make you happy.

The menu includes the best cracklins'. They are hot, salty, spicy, and fatty—the perfect combination to give you energy for thinking about what else to order. Much of the meat here is slow-cooked cuts that are full of flavor. That means such cuts as lamb neck or confit of this meat or that. Chef Isaac has been influenced greatly by his two Cajun grandmothers, and you can see the loving attention to the food at the Meatery. Grilled artichokes, fried rabbit livers, venison, quail, and other meats that you might not see in other restaurants reflect Chef Isaac's Cajun roots. He's even published a cookbook celebrating this last

Left: Bone marrow.

Right: Grilled artichokes.

stronghold of regional American called *Chasing the Gator: Isaac Toups and the New Cajun Cooking,* which he co-authored with journalist Jennifer V. Cole. Inside it you'll find more than one hundred of his mouthwatering recipes.

Even the cocktails here are delicious and full flavored. The bar at Toups' Meatery has a deep selection of ryes, bourbons, and other spirits. There are new and interesting cocktails. And there is a wine list that is extraordinary from this jewel box of a restaurant. Pairing wines for dinner with the often spicy and distinctly seasoned house specialties is not a challenge because of the wine list, including a variety of sparkling wines.

Dessert? These desserts are generous and delicious. Between the doberge cake and the cheese board or the after dinner drinks, you will not leave wanting.

845 N. Carrollton Ave.
New Orleans, LA
504-252-4999
toupsmeatery.com

DAKOTA

A trip across Lake Pontchartrain for a dining adventure

Dakota Restaurant is located in the city of Covington on the north shore of Lake Pontchartrain. Eating in this place requires a trip to the suburbs, but it is definitely worth it. The city of Covington is charming, with an active arts scene and many interesting restaurants. Even among those, Dakota stands out. Chef/owner Kim Kringlie has created a contemporary Louisiana restaurant, which uses fresh local produce, as well as the best fish from the waters near the city alongside poultry and meat. It's named after the chef's state of birth: North Dakota. He moved to Louisiana in 1983 to work in Baton Rouge with famous Cajun chef, John Folse. He opened Dakota in 1990 after absorbing the techniques and flavors of Louisiana.

The restaurant is definitely a white tablecloth establishment, but is casually elegant with excellent service. The restaurant is open for lunch and dinner. Lunch offerings are lighter and smaller, but offer the same degree of elegance as the more formal evening fare. The small plates at lunch will be a great shared meal. The charbroiled oysters are seasoned two ways, either with a truffle parmesan butter or with a bacon and bleu cheese butter. You can't go wrong. Shrimp and grits can be a small plate. Tuna bites, lamb nachos, or a charcuterie plate are also good choices.

The crabmeat and Brie soup is the signature dish of the restaurant. You should not pass it up. The Dakota salad is served with Asiago cheese and mixed greens. There's a lump crabmeat sandwich, which is grilled and served with cheese that melts obligingly to hold the crab in the bread. The bacon and blue cheese burger is served with tomato jam on a brioche bun, while the pulled pork sandwich (actually a panini) is made with pulled pork, three cheeses, and greens. In this day and age where sandwiches are becoming gourmet items in and of themselves, the sandwiches from Dakota are on the cutting edge.

Moving to large plates, the crab still does not stop. A crab and shrimp stuffed avocado may seem like an old-fashioned entrée, but in the hands of Chef Kim, it is definitely modern. There is always a fish of the day. And the New York strip steak is served with the traditional wedge of iceberg lettuce. You can have liver and onions, a steak frites, or a Caesar salad with fried oysters. There's a green bean amandine that is very good and an excellent macaroni and cheese.

At night, besides the lunch offerings, you can get foie gras and pork belly. The salad called the Bleu is made with mixed greens, apples, and a bleu cheese vinaigrette. You can get a whole-roasted flounder with caramelized onions, fennel, and olives. Puppy drum is topped with lump crab meat. And the lamb chops are served with feta, beet hummus, and a mint chimichurri.

For dessert you may choose a white chocolate brownie, which is magic on the tongue. The coconut cake is really tasty and served with a crème Anglaise. There is a banana split for those who are still hungry enough to order it, served with house-made ice creams, and topped with fruit and caramel and chocolate sauces.

The wine list is mostly American and very well suited to the menu. There are good wines by the glass, beer, and house cocktails. If you do eat at the bar, many of the delicious appetizers and snacks are available. Definitely worth the trip across the lake.

629 N. Hwy. 190
Covington, LA
985-892-3712
thedakotarestaurant.com

PIZZA DELICIOUS

New York pizza and more in New Orleans

Chef owners Mike Friedman and Greg Augarten were college roommates in New Orleans from New York who missed pizza—that crisp, thin-crusted New York pizza. Eventually all their complaining turned to brainstorming when they realized that maybe they could actually bring the taste they craved to New Orleans. So in their homesick condition, they began to putter around in an industrial kitchen, trying to reproduce their taste memories by trial and error.

When they felt they were ready, they began to offer pizza, but just on Sundays. You ordered online and picked up your pizza by walking down an alley. This was a regular pop-up affair, but everyone loved it. All that was missing in this clandestine operation was a secret knock. They went from once a week, to twice a week, and then to a real operation with a kitchen and a restaurant. The rest is history, as they say. Pizza Delicious began to operate on a regular basis, and the city discovered that it was so hungry for New York pizza that Greg and Mike were an immediate success. They now just keep improving by expanding their offerings—beyond pizza. They make regular trips to Italy to explore the food, flavors, and techniques of that country.

Of course, the real star here is the pizza, selected as the best pizza in New Orleans by a panel assembled by nola.com. They don't make their sauce too sweet; there isn't too much cheese. Choices include cheese, pepperoni, and the margherita. There's also a vegetable pizza, and a Hawaiian pizza made interesting with sriracha. Need some side dishes? Try the garlic knots: they're addictive. There's also a vegan pasta, bucatini carbonara, and changing pasta offerings. The salads like the Caesar and the house salad are freshly made. For dessert there are three types of cookies, and not always the same ones. There is wine and beer. Not a long list, but this is a pizza joint after all, albeit an unconventional one.

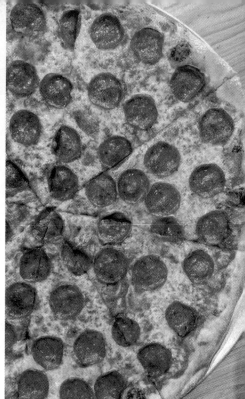

Top left: Outside Pizza Delicious.
Bottom left: Famous garlic knots.
Right: Pizza.

Pizza Delicious draws people from all over the city, but those who live in the Marigny/Bywater area have access to limited delivery in the evenings. That may be important if you are staying in the area.

617 Piety St.
New Orleans, LA
504-676-8482
pizzadelicious.com

SUCRÉ

A modern patisserie with national impact

What could serve as a sweeter harbinger of the Carnival season than a shimmery ring of purple, green, and gold king cake covered in edible glitter? Sucré means sugar and the nationally recognized bakery has become synonymous with its favorite ingredient. While its king cake shines (literally) at Mardi Gras, its other treats have earned it loyal customers throughout the year and from all parts of the United States where it ships its goods within a few business days.

Sucré is a coffee shop that serves ice cream, coffee, tea, and a plethora of baked delicacies for your decadent pleasure. The treats are artisan made and sit like little jewels on your plate. Besides the retail pastry shop that is Sucré, there is also the sit-down restaurant where the treats can be enjoyed with a cup of coffee. The gelato is outstanding, and the restaurant and shop are visually stunning. The brass, copper, and iron touches that pervade the shops make it as French leaning, but New York modern in both look and feel.

The beautiful shops, at two locations, offer gelati, macarons, chocolates, and pastries both for sale to take away (in their signature boxes and bags) and to eat in the beautiful space. All of the teas and coffees are locally sourced. The national retail component of Sucré sometimes overshadows the coffee shop and pastry aspect of the

The king cake celebrates the beginning of the Carnival season. They are eaten beginning on Twelfth Night–January 6–until Mardi Gras, each year. After Mardi Gras the citizens of New Orleans wait patiently for king cakes to arrive again the following January 6. Inside each cake is a small plastic favor, usually a baby. The person whose piece of cake includes the baby either must buy the next king cake or–if it is a party–is the king or queen of the party.

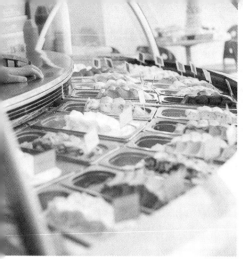

Left: Gelato. Credit: Sam Hanna.
Right: Macaron. Credit: Sam Hanna.

place, but to forget the pleasure of sitting and enjoying the delightful concoctions in house, whether with a slice of cake, a dish of gelato, a cookie, or a plate of macarons, would be a mistake. After all, Tariq Hanna, the former executive pastry chef, was named Pastry Chef of the Year by *New Orleans* magazine. He and Joel Dondis conceived of a French patisserie with such a stellar reputation that its goodies would be sought by people all over the country. When you eat there, you can let your taste buds be the judge of their success.

During the Mardi Gras season, the special king cake developed by Sucré with its gold leaf embellished pastry is not to be missed. The pastry is lightly flavored with cinnamon and is buttery and rich. It also contains that very New Orleans specialty, Creole cream cheese. This cake does nod a bit to the other traditional colors of purple and green, but it screams gold. In 2011 the *Washington Post* named this the city's best king cake.

3025 Magazine St.
New Orleans, LA
504-520-8311

622 Conti St.
New Orleans, LA
504-267-7098

shopsucre.com

CENTRAL GROCERY

A bit of Sicily in old New Orleans

Around the turn of the nineteenth century, New Orleans became the new home for almost 300,000 immigrants of Italian descent fleeing political turmoil back home. Meanwhile, the urban scene in New Orleans was shifting and the French Quarter was largely emptied out as residents favored newly minted Uptown. The new arrivals, many of them Sicilian, moved in and the new area of "Little Palermo," named after Sicily's capital, was born. Italian groceries and restaurants popped up and new traditions—like St. Joseph's Day altars—would begin to leave their indelible mark on the city forever.

A trip to New Orleans that fails to explore the deep Sicilian food influences on the city is a real mistake. One of those iconic places to experience the Sicilian influence is Central Grocery. The store was founded in 1906 by Salvatore Lupo, a Sicilian immigrant. It is still operated by his descendants. It was opened in the Little Palermo section of the French Quarter, at the time heavily populated by Sicilians. That meant that the demand for products from Sicily, especially food products, was high. And Central Grocery was opened to cater to the needs of these new citizens.

This is the place that claims to have invented the muffuletta—an Italian sandwich piled high with house-sliced Italian cold cuts, Italian cheeses, and their family olive salad. The name muffuletta is the name of the round loaf of bread covered in sesame seeds that serves as the base for the sandwich. Even today you can find muffuletta loaves sold at bakeries in Sicily.

There is a back counter where you can enjoy the massive sandwich—or share one—as well as buy jars of olive salad and many other Italian products from the shop. You can eat the sandwich outside in Jackson Square, sitting on a bench and enjoying the day. Or finish it later in

The mighty muffuletta. Credit: Scott Ott Creative.

your hotel room. The longer that olive oil is allowed to soak into the bread, the better. And it's also a store that sells its own souvenirs, like the family cookbook and aprons.

Central Grocery is open every day, so there's no need to worry about your muffuletta craving raising its head at the wrong time. Central Grocery doesn't offer you many additional options; they're making what they know. And they know muffulettas. Don't think that you can eat a whole one. Sharing a half of a sandwich is probably a good plan.

923 Decatur St.
New Orleans, LA
504-523-1620
centralgrocery.com

BYWATER AMERICAN BISTRO

A restaurant that celebrates the food of America

Bywater is one of the hip neighborhoods of New Orleans. It's an old neighborhood full of vintage Spanish and French-style homes that are being rediscovered by young couples, artists, and bohemians. Nestled in the neighborhood is the New Orleans Center for the Creative Arts (NOCCA) and not far away is Bywater American Bistro. The restaurant serves a neighborhood that is full of diversity and interesting architecture alongside its famous colorful murals.

The food reflects the diversity of experience in the kitchen and the great variety of local foods. There is inspiration in the freshness of ingredients from local farms and fisheries. Chef Levi Raines, the longtime sous chef at Compère Lapin, is helming the kitchen. This is a restaurant of Chef Nina Compton and her husband and partner, Larry Miller.

Chef Compton is from San Lucia. She and Larry Miller, have made New Orleans their new home. The flavors of the city and its steamy atmosphere appealed to them, with its reflections of the Caribbean. Nina is a *Top Chef* star who spent some of her training years in Italy. She operated a fine dining restaurant in a restaurant in the Warehouse District. Conceived with long-time and trusted sous chef, Levi Raines,

NOCCA is the school of the arts in New Orleans. Besides the traditional classes in dance, creative writing, music, drama, and art, the school considers the culinary arts one of the arts on par with the others. The program pulls students from the greater New Orleans area to learn from a program put together by the culinary school at Johnson & Wales.

the trio has created a restaurant that reflects a bit of the Caribbean side of the city, as well as its very American side. All of this is wrapped up in the relaxed atmosphere that is so much a reflection of America today. They have managed to make this place trendy and homey at the same time.

The dinner menu has some delicious light appetizers, including the tomatillo gazpacho, pickled shrimp, and cobia escabeche with fennel and radish. The rest of the menu depends on your mood. Pasta? Try the pasta with tomato sauce. Curried snapper with green apple and sticky rice is not the least bit traditional, but oh so good. There is a jerk chicken rice and a farro risotto with mushrooms. Vegetables include okra, squash, potato, and cabbage—also not your typical restaurant vegetables.

Want half a chicken? It's on the menu. And so is pork belly with apple and wild rice and duck breast with figs and butter beans. There is great creativity in the menu and in the execution. It's pretty special for a neighborhood restaurant. This menu is not for the unadventurous. It's one that serves a special neighborhood with a diverse population. It's informal, airy, and not a place with pretense or fussiness. Rather, it exudes creativity and innovation.

Brunch brings you a corndog, smoke tuna toast, or fruit salad. There is rice porridge and shrimp or an omelet and salad. There is what's called a "proper breakfast" with boudin noir—blood sausage—on the plate. It is a really special breakfast plate. There's smoked brisket with a soft scramble. French toast with rum caramel and banana provides a sweeter breakfast option, or try a dessert like the banana split or Nutella flan.

The cocktail menu is fun and very much in line with the quirkiness and deliciousness of the entire menu. And of course, the bar can make traditional cocktails, too.

2900 Chartres St.
New Orleans, LA
504-605-3827
bywateramericanbistro.com

MOPHO

The Creolization of Vietnamese food

The story of MoPho's founding is as intrinsic to New Orleans as the very pantry it uses to make its delicious Southeast Asian inspired cuisine. According to its founders, it was late at night; they were craving the popular Vietnamese soup pho, but had nowhere to buy it. Since one of those hungry revelers just happened to be a chef, the progression to opening their own pho restaurant was a natural and, in this case, almost immediate next step. They inquired into renting space at the restaurant's current home the very next day.

Chef Michael Gulotta and his cofounders have watched the restaurant take off, winning awards like the 2014 *New Orleans* magazine's Restaurant of the Year and himself lauded as one of the Best New Chefs of 2016 by *Food & Wine* magazine. The concept was simple enough, but the result is food with complexity and myriad layers of texture and flavor.

Chef Michael insists that the pronunciation of the restaurant's name—pronounced "Moe Foe" and certainly winking at a more profane interpretation—is just as New Orleans as the restaurant itself. After years working at the fanciest white tablecloth restaurants, he has created a restaurant with paper towels, no linens, and a dressed-down menu with food that is recognizable, yet astonishingly delicious. He has created food that is accessible and affordable, while exceeding expectations.

MoPho offers lunch starters that are crisp and seasoned with peanut and cilantro. It also offers po'boys, which are a cross between the traditional New Orleans po'boy and the Vietnamese banh mi with traditional Vietnamese pickled vegetables instead of the New Orleans vinegar choices. Curry, turmeric, and kimchi flavored chicken and dumplings, fried oysters, and duck round out the lunch menu.

Left: Pepper jelly clams.
Right: Pho.

At night for dinner, choose pho, made as a vegetarian version or with bone marrow or fowl. But inside that pho might be hog's head cheese or meatballs. The fun of it and its delicious flavor make you forget that it's anything but expected. With beer, a small yet interesting wine list, and a very interesting cocktail list, you will happily explore the entire menu—from food to drink. There are a number of wines available by the glass.

There are definitely traditions that have been worked into the fabric of MoPho. On Thursdays, MoPho celebrates vegetables. Saturdays it celebrates whole roasted pig. Knowing where to find tasty vegetarian dishes that actually taste good is always good information to have in your back pocket and MoPho revels in vegetables. Eat there when you need a place that can accommodate vegetarians in a tasty way, while not disappointing the rest of your party.

514 City Park Ave.
New Orleans, LA
504-482-6845
mophonola.com

BON TON CAFÉ

A traditional Cajun restaurant in New Orleans

There was a time when the Bon Ton was not only the best Cajun restaurant in the city, it was the only Cajun restaurant in the city. It has developed such a following over the years that it is able to set its own rules. The restaurant was opened in 1953 by Al and Alzina Pearce, and it has been sharing its Cajun flavors with several generations. It is definitely old school. The tablecloths are checkered, red and white. The recipes are based on family recipes and served that way. There is nothing "chef-ish" about presentation, which makes the food seem even more authentic. The staff has been there forever, ensuring a continuity with the past that is loved by the citizens of New Orleans.

When the Pearces began preparing Cajun food in this bastion of Creole cuisine, diners were not used to eating crawfish etoufée or crawfish bisque. Foods like shrimp and crab were familiar to local diners, but crawfish was a particular Cajun delicacy that was not usually available at restaurants in New Orleans. That changed in the 1970s as crawfish farming began to produce crawfish in sufficient volume to make a reliable supply for restaurants in New Orleans. The Cajun preparation of the "mudbug" in various dishes would take its time making its way to New Orleans tables.

So what's good? What's authentic? The thinly sliced, fried catfish is a fresh and perfect presentation. The Bon Ton was the only place to find crawfish bisque reliably on a restaurant menu; it was something that was often available in people's homes, but not in restaurants. The Bon Ton still has crawfish bisque on the menu. Order it. Made with chopped crawfish in a cornbread dressing and stuffed back into the head of the crawfish, it's served in an intensely flavored broth. The fried crawfish appetizer is also delightful. The crawfish jambalaya is really different from traditional New Orleans jambalaya and worth a taste, especially as a standard for comparison.

Crabmeat and onion rings.

The menu is heavy with fresh fish for a reason—it's good. Most of the preparations are part of the simple presentation of authentic Cajun food. Fresh Gulf fish—available seasonally—embellished with oysters or shrimp is on offer. The redfish and the speckled trout are hallmarks of the Cajun fishermen.

The rum Ramsey, the signature cocktail of the restaurant, is still prepared from the secret recipe. The bread pudding with whiskey sauce is their signature dessert, originally reflecting the frugal nature of the Cajun kitchen. There is an à la mode option for the bread pudding. Choose that. You might as well gild the lily.

The restaurant serves lunch and dinner, Monday through Friday. Especially for the evening meal, you should consider making reservations. The wine list is adequate, but you're going there for the food. And if you're looking for weekend dining, this isn't the place. The Bon Ton Café is successful enough that it can reserve weekends for itself.

401 Magazine St.
New Orleans, LA
504-524-3386
thebontoncafe.com

SOBOU

A spirited restaurant south of Bourbon Street

SoBou calls itself a spirited restaurant. And it is—both in ambiance and its healthy admiration for alcoholic spirits. After all, their capable team boasts both a "Cocktail Chick" (Ti Adelaide Martin) and a "Wine Guy" (Dan Davis) at the helm. Although it is a restaurant, it's very bar forward, so that not only cocktails, but also other bar service is really encouraged in a tasteful way. The food is designed to support and enhance the drinking so that the bar chefs can produce the best and tastiest drinks. Created by the team from Commander's Palace, including members of the famous Brennan family, its name is derived from its location south of Bourbon street. Thoughtful consideration is given to bridge ingredients, meaning that Ti and the team are constantly pairing the food with cocktails, as well as wine and beer. It's the place you can go to drink cocktails with your meal without anyone looking askance

You cannot rely on the online listings at SoBou because the team there is constantly experimenting and it is nothing but fun to go there and see what's happening. You can always expect a soup du jour and a gumbo du jour. Just wait and see what is on offer. The shrimp beignets are made to be dipped in New Orleans–style barbecue sauce. There is a watermelon gazpacho, tacos, tamales, and a wonderful peach and grape salad.

The barbecued brisket is served with corn on the cob and pickled vegetables. Yellowfin tuna is served with Louisiana caviar in blood orange juice. There is a crispy whole fish that is designed to be shared. And there is a very Cuban-inspired ropa vieja.

Dessert is surprising and yet another chance to indulge in a creative cocktail. The chocolate-covered crackling served with peanut butter–flavored whipped cream is called Pecan Pie, Not Pie. The white

Left: Foie gras apple pie.
Right: Surf and turf.

chocolate bread pudding is served with cherries jubilee. All of these delights taste wonderful with spirits or some other liquor, and SoBou is prepared for you to enjoy them.

The house cocktails are reasonably priced and inventive. Of course, the traditional cocktails are also available. The wines by the glass come in three-ounce and six-ounce pours, which gives you a great deal of control as a consumer. And the beer offerings are quite extensive.

310 Chartres St.
New Orleans, LA
504-522-4095
sobounola.com

SAC-A-LAIT

A modernist eating establishment with country roots

Sac-a-Lait has won many awards and been recognized as a very respectful and imaginative farm-to-table and fresh seafood restaurant. The menu reflects it. The tastes and flavors produced by the husband and wife owner/duo, Cody and Samantha Carroll, are innovative and inventive. The restaurant is set in the old Cotton Mill building in the Warehouse District in New Orleans. The restaurant is a family affair, and the whole family has helped craft the details of the building with as much care as the menu. The raw bar is made with crushed shell, for example. The decor is a combination of iron and wood. Sac-a-Lait was named Restaurant of the Year in 2015 by *New Orleans* magazine. It was recognized by *Travel & Leisure* magazine as the Best Farm to Table Restaurant in Louisiana. Open Table included it in its list of 100 Best Restaurants for Foodies. The chefs were named Kings of Louisiana Seafood in 2013, winning the seafood cook-off.

Since the menu changes seasonally, this description can only hint at what a diner might encounter at Sac-a-Lait, but be prepared for something that surprises you and also sounds inviting. Redfish, oyster, crab, and snapper may be offered. They are all fresh and tasty served with vegetables, which are both cultivated and foraged. The restaurant distinguishes between hunted meat and farmed meat. So under the hunt menu there might be alligator, duck, frog, and deer. On the farm side might be pig, crawfish, or veal.

> The Carrolls have another restaurant in New Roads called Hot Tails that's housed in an old drive-through convenience store. It's the more laid-back of their restaurants, focusing on "hardcore" south Louisiana cuisine like po'boys and craft cocktails.

Left: Alligator and mirliton.
Center: Tableside duck gumbo.
Right: Redfish and okra.

Be prepared for an adventure when eating here. The menu is not traditional. It sometimes verges on edgy, pushing the diner to try something new—either in preparation or in the type of food presented. You might be prepared to eat veal brains, for example. Once something that was eaten regularly, today eating brains is an out-of-the-ordinary selection. It is, however, delicious. And in serving it, the Carrolls are making the statement that the entire animal should be eaten, not just the muscle meat with which we are all familiar. You'll find some unchallenging dishes on the menu, too, so don't be put off by the unusual ingredients. This is a modern restaurant with real attempts to serve special, thoughtful food, not just good food. Each dish is really prepared à la minute. It does depend on the luxury of a pot of gumbo, a pot of red beans, or a pot of turtle soup.

The venison and duck are particularly well handled. The use of duck fat to flavor and crisp potatoes is a wonderful touch, both from a taste perspective and to further the practice of using the whole animal.

The cocktail program is just as carefully planned with natural and foraged ingredients as the rest of the menu. Visit Sac-a-Lait and experience the creativity and intense respect for the ingredients that makes the food both sensually satisfying and intellectually compelling.

1051 Annunciation
New Orleans, LA
504-324-3658
sac-a-laitrestaurant.com

CAFÉ DEGAS

A bit of France on the historic French boulevard

With nearly a century between them, two French artists have graced this section of Esplanade Avenue with their talent and love for the Crescent City. The first, Edgar Degas, came to visit family in New Orleans before returning to Paris to become one of the icons of the Impressionist movement. The second, Jacques Soulas, together with Jerry Edgar would create a French restaurant in Degas's very footsteps and named in his honor.

The lovely French restaurant serving café fare on Esplanade Avenue near the New Orleans Museum of Art has grown over the years. The tiny building first expanded with an open-air covered deck. Then it created walls around the decking to expand seating even in winter or when the rain is coming in sideways. The restaurant is really French in values and in menu. The restaurant is open for lunch between Wednesday and Friday, brunch on Saturday and Sunday, and dinner Wednesday through Sunday.

Lunch regularly includes mussels, snails, and cheeses. The restaurant serves a mean French onion soup and a lovely crab salad. Hangar steak, liver and onions, and salad Niçoise round out the choices. Many of the same dishes can be found at night, as well as veal medallions and lamb.

During the 1880s Edgar Degas visited his brother and cousins from his mother's family who lived in New Orleans. The house is the only house where Degas lived that is open to the public. The Musson family lived on the oak-lined Esplanade Avenue in a house built before the Civil War. It offers tours with an emphasis on the rooms where Degas lived. It's now a bed and breakfast and a venue for parties and receptions.

Left: Floating island.
Right: The patio is magical at night.

The pasta dishes are very delicate. There is always a vegetarian special, which makes Café Degas an important place to remember when looking for a vegetarian meal. An à la carte vegetable selection includes Brussels sprouts, haricots verts, and asparagus.

Café Degas is the place to go for a late lunch or an early dinner after a day of exploring the arts at the New Orleans Museum of Art and at Degas House. The tiny early restaurant opened in 1980. It was a restaurant that in spirit reflected—and still does—the combination of a real Frenchman and an American with the result being a very New Orleans place. Visit the Degas paintings at MOMA, painted while he visited his brother, and the house where he stayed when he visited the city. Sitting on the deck eating a lovely crab salad before a trip to the museum is a lovely experience. When you're eating at Café Degas, you feel transported from your everyday life and can relax with a lovely meal; you can appreciate quiet atmosphere that Café Degas offers.

3127 Esplanade Ave.
New Orleans, LA
504-945-5635
cafedegas.com

BISTRO ORLEANS

A bright New Orleans bistro in Metairie

One of the certainties of living and dining in the greater New Orleans area is that when it comes to a restaurant, you can never predict its deliciousness by its location. That's certainly the case with Bistro Orleans, tucked away in Metairie with only an unassuming blue canopy to set it apart from the other tenants.

Inside, above the Oldies music soundtrack, you can hear the sizzling sound of a dozen charbroiled oysters on a hot platter coming out of the kitchen before being able to see or smell them. It's a pleasant sound indeed, that announces the imminent arrival of an order of "Oysters Esplanade," a delicious blend of grilled oysters on the half shell piled high with melted applewood bacon and pepper jack cheese. Once, restaurants of this caliber dotted the New Orleans landscape from the Lakefront to the CBD to Uptown and beyond. Today, a find like Bistro Orleans is a satisfying reminder that quality is still valued, especially when it comes to a good meal.

The chef and owner, Archie Saurage, born and raised in New Orleans, has put together an unbelievably tempting menu of traditional New Orleans, classic Italian cuisine, and an impressive steak selection that's a throwback to traditional neighborhood restaurants all over the city. The moderate prices are another bonus, in line with what you would expect from most restaurants of this genre.

Chef Saurage knows how to charbroil an oyster without making it too hard, and the seasonings are delightful. Order the "Classic

Metairie and Lakeview both border Lake Pontchartrain. Seafood restaurants used to dot the shoreline, with some very casual places located on pilings over the lake. Bistro Orleans reminds you of one of those old-time joints—with the notable addition of air-conditioning.

Fish amandine over pasta.

Charbroiled" topped with oysters in a garlic butter and Parmesan, served with a generous helping of perfectly toasted French bread.

For an entrée, choose one that is right at home in this friendly dining room and often hard to find in today's restaurant scene—twin stuffed crabs with sides of crisp coleslaw, creamy potato salad, and a huge order of onion rings. You'll see that the crabs arrive not in some ceramic dish, but rather in freshly stuffed crab shells. The dish is perfectly toasted and crunchy on the outside with a generous combination of crabmeat and breading inside. Its spicy familiar ingredients bring back delicious memories of leisurely Sunday lunches.

Perhaps the most memorable dish is an incredibly rich, creamy, delicate-yet-full-flavored cheese, corn, and seafood bisque fresh from the stove to the table. Ladled straight from the pot, it will only get better as it simmers on the stove for a few more hours for the lucky diners that follow you for dinner.

So, if you want a deliciously unpretentious, traditional New Orleans–style meal with all the local and Italian dishes you love from long ago, don't judge a strip mall restaurant by its cover, and head over to Bistro Orleans for a satisfying meal.

3216 W. Esplanade Ave.
Metairie, LA
504-304-1469
bistroorleansmetairie.com

FIVE HAPPINESS

Really good Chinese food in Mid-City New Orleans

Trendy restaurants often come and go, but the true classics stick around. Five Happiness has been a consistent favorite among the local crowd in Mid-City for the last forty years, and has even been named the Best Chinese Restaurant in the whole city by *New Orleans* magazine and *Gambit*. The key to its success has been its ability to present a variety of Chinese dishes from various regions while still appealing to the unique tastes of its Crescent City customers.

This restaurant doesn't shy away from being pan Chinese, offering specialties from many regions of China. Yet it has some easy choices for those who are not experienced eaters from the Chinese palate. The shrimp with honey-roasted pecans, for example, is very Chinese in its presentation and methodology, but is made with local ingredients, which makes the flavors easy on the palates of locals. Another excellent house special is chicken with asparagus. And the house-roasted duck is outstanding. The stuffed Chinese eggplant—full of shrimp and pork— is related to, but different from Creole stuffed eggplant, emphasizing the parallels to the food of Louisiana.

The restaurant feels busy all of the time, with a bustle of wait staff and the constant moving in and out of customers. It is has been run by Paggy Lee since she moved from California to New Orleans in 1978. Ms. Lee is deeply involved with the local community. She is a member of the Mystic Krewe of Nyx, an all-woman Mardi Gras krewe, and even served as the super krewe's grand marshal for 2016. She makes the restaurant appealing and welcoming for all customers.

As an appetizer, pot stickers are excellent, as are the dishes with vegetables such as beef with string beans. All of the food at Five Happiness is made on site. The menu looks very much like other

The Guardian of Five Happiness.

Chinese restaurant menus, with dishes that are familiar; however, the food is not premade and the dishes are well prepared and tasty.

The food is delicious and really superior to expectations. If you can sit around the perimeter of the room, a bit away from the hustle and bustle of the service, you can enjoy good Chinese food, actually prepared on site, and with a bit of leisure and room for conversation. The restaurant will also prepare something special for you and your guests if you call ahead. The bar is not innovative, but it can make traditional drinks.

3605 S. Carrollton Ave.
New Orleans, LA
504-482-3935
fivehappiness.com

RALPH'S ON THE PARK

Lunch and dinner on City Park

Located across the street from historic City Park, Ralph's on the Park allows you to walk among hundred-year-old oaks, take a swan boat on the lagoons, and then finish your evening with a special dinner. Over its nearly 160-year history, this space has hosted fine dining establishments from some of New Orleans's most hallowed restaurateurs. After operating as a coffee house from 1860 to 1893, the building was bought by Fernand Alciatore, a son of Antoine—yes, that Antoine—Alciatore. Fernand operated A La Renaissance des Chenes Verts, one of the city's best restaurants, until 1901, when he sold the space to Justin Tujague—yes, that Tujague—who catered, among other clientele, to the working women of Storyville, New Orleans's famous red-light district.

Today, Ralph's on the Park is owned by Ralph Brennan—yes, well, you know—who insists on the finest farm- and sea-to-table cuisine from New Orleans native son Chef Chip Flanagan. Serving lunch Tuesday through Friday, dinner every night, and an elegant brunch on weekends, Ralph's menus, from bar to brunch, are globally inspired but most definitely infused with local flavor.

The two-course lunch includes a salad or soup of the day as a starter with a choice of crawfish pasta, buttermilk fried chicken sandwich, or the daily special. If you order à la carte, there are even more choices. Plates of fried oyster, shrimp, or garlic bread can be shared at the table. Roasted beet salad, tuna tartare, or even the City Park salad are excellent choices. Crawfish, fish, or steak are great options for lunch.

At dinner there are several soups, oysters, various vegetables, and various meats including beef, rabbit, and pork. As always in New Orleans, there is lots of seafood on the menu. Ralph's offers a serious vegetarian option that is about flavor and not at all a sacrifice. And the menu really does embrace the traditions of New Orleans—there is a ya-ka mein on the menu. The menu is full of New Orleans standbys, but

Top: A shared baked fish.

Left: Outstanding plating makes the appetizers even more inviting.

the menu is not boring and the flavors of the dishes are fresh. Somehow the kitchen manages to make those traditional foods really new and modern while not scaring away tradition-bound New Orleans eaters.

Desserts are serious. A cheese plate, banana bread pudding, and chocolate doberge cake are some of the heavy hitters. The flourless chocolate cake is a delightful end to your meal. The wine list is very broad, with lots of by-the-glass choices, and the cocktail program is lively and varied.

900 City Park Ave.
New Orleans, LA
504-488-1000
ralphsonthepark.com

Home of the Black Duck Bar

The Palace Café opened in 1991 in the completely transformed Werlein's Music Store, retrofitting the space to preserve a treasured building on Canal Street. Inside this modern temple to traditional Creole food, you'll also find a rum-loving bar popular enough to house the New Orleans Rum Society.

Sugarcane has always been a staple of New Orleans's economy, ever since it was first introduced in 1751. So it's no wonder that rum became such an important spirit in the city when it was discovered that you could produce it by using the byproducts from sugar refinement. The Black Duck Bar even honors the city's signature spirit in its name—after one of the fastest rum-running ships that evaded capture during Prohibition until a tenacious Coast Guard captain ended its days as a smuggling vessel. While most of its crew didn't survive its capture, the violence sparked debate that would eventually lead to an end to Prohibition and the resurgence of rum as a part of legitimate commerce and culture in New Orleans. Joining the New Orleans Rum Society at the Black Duck Bar is free and offers members the chance to try new rums and fill up their own "rum passport."

The restaurant recognizes the need for good bar food for snacking alongside all that rum. Fried duck wings and good cheese support the cocktail program. The crabmeat cheesecake is a dish associated with Palace Café. It's a creamy, savory homage to crabmeat and cheese. The shrimp remoulade is classic, but presented in a modern way. Salads can allow you to eat lightly, but entrées from seafood to shrimp to hamburgers are on offer at lunch. Dinner also allows you to choose from a light meal to a real hearty steak. The choices are definitely Creole and traditional, but also modern. Shrimp Tchefuncte—Gulf shrimp in meunière sauce with mushrooms and rice—is an example of modern Creole food. Andouille-crusted fish is another example. And pepper-crusted duck is yet another. Creole bouillabaisse is a classic

Left: Shrimp Tchefuncte.
Center: Eggs Benedict.
Right: Andouille-crusted fish.

Creole dish that has been updated, including Gulf fish, crab meat, and shrimp in a tomato broth.

Salads like the Werlein salad, named for the former owners of the building, have become classic at Palace Café. The Werlein is a twist on the Caesar salad. The wedge is made with green goddess dressing, a nod at former chefs in New Orleans. And turtle soup, gumbo, or the soup du jour can complete a meal at Palace Café.

For dessert try white chocolate bread pudding, cheesecake, or crème brûlée. A favorite is rum pineapple doberge cake. The wine list, including wines by the glass, is extensive, and the spirits in the bar are deep.

The restaurant is open for breakfast and brunch, so remember that when you are wondering where to eat early in the morning. Enjoy a jazz brunch there in the New Orleans tradition every Saturday and Sunday. Or try a sing-along brunch during the holidays.

The restaurant has been honored with the *Wine Spectator* Award—a good sign that the wine offerings at Palace Café are excellent. There are many wines offered by the glass, in many categories. The fortified and sweet wine selections are also extensive. The fortified wines go well with the excellent charcuterie that the Black Duck Bar serves.

605 Canal St.
New Orleans, LA
504-523-1661
palacecafe.com

COMPÈRE LAPIN

A little bit of the Caribbean in downtown New Orleans

Chef Nina Compton and her husband and partner, Larry Miller, have created a Caribbean-inspired restaurant that melds seamlessly with the foods of New Orleans. The restaurant is named for Brother Rabbit, who is a wily character in the folklore of the Caribbean and the Americas. Like any good folk tale character, Compère Lapin is mischievous and fun loving, but still manages to convey a moral lesson or an explanation of the natural world. Chef Nina read these clever tales as a child and brings the same spirit of jaunty exploration to the restaurant she named after them.

The spice profile, though unique to the islands, reminds the diner of the many connections between the Creole and island cuisines. Most memorable is the attention to detail and the beautiful presentation. The restaurant is very open in an industrial-style renovation with brick walls, stone floors, and windows full of light located in the Old No. 77 Hotel & Chandlery.

Chef Nina Compton has been recognized by the James Beard Foundation, received many awards and much recognition, and done her stint on *Top Chef.* But she is carefully focused on the food.

The restaurant is open for lunch, dinner, and brunch. The tables are placed to allow for conversation and conviviality. The dishes are straightforward and yet complex in flavor profile and in nuanced execution. Conch croquettes, curried goat, and jerk black drum reflect the islands. Gnocchi and pastas reflect Chef Compton's experience working in Italian restaurants. And the fresh seafood is grounded deeply in the food of New Orleans. Eating here is a wonderful dining experience—recognized by the James Beard Foundation. It is a place for celebration with imaginative food served beautifully.

The food is definitely not the traditional food of New Orleans, which adds to the experience of dining here. For example, spiced pig ears is

Roasted jerk corn with smoked mayo. Credit: Sara Essex Bradley.

different but delicious. The crispy dirty rice arancini is a bridge between modernity and tradition. You can get a half of roasted chicken with deliciously spiced skin or black drum with cauliflower and summer squash. Try the pork tenderloin with okra and plantain crema.

Desserts are also true to the Caribbean. Soursop semifreddo and coconut panna cotta are perfect for the weather in New Orleans, reflect the flavors of the Caribbean, and at the same time also reveal Chef Nina's Italian cooking background. The spiced chocolate mousse is full of surprises like cashews. There are house-made ice creams and sorbets. And the roasted banana zeppole with hazelnut and rum caramel is a wonderful end to a meal. There are some lovely dessert wines and fortified wines to drink with your dessert. If you're in the mood for a stiff drink with which to end the meal, there are flights of whiskey.

The cocktail program at Compère Lapin is wonderful and inventive. The house cocktails are really fun and tasty, but the bar is well schooled in the traditional cocktails. And the list of amari, absinthe, and brandies is really remarkable. Ask for a traditional absinthe drip while you are sitting at the bar. It is certainly possible to have bar snacks from the menu while you sip your cocktails. The beer list is very extensive, so if you are a beer lover, skip wine and pair those Caribbean flavors with beer. That is a perfect combination. There are extensive choices of wine by the glass. No matter what your preference, you will be happy.

535 Tchoupitoulas St.
New Orleans, LA
504-599-2199
comperelapin.com

STEAMBOAT *NATCHEZ*

A dining room floating down the river

Not every place to eat is on land. Floating down the river on a real steamboat while you enjoy your meal on the steamboat *Natchez* allows you to be part of the history of the river. The steam engine was built in the early twentieth century, and the *Natchez* is the last authentic one still cruising the Mississippi River. The *Natchez* is equipped with a real steam calliope (traditional pipe organ) whose jaunty sounds are a throwback to another time. The captain still gives his orders through a megaphone. And as you glide through the water watching that wheel turn in the water, you will also see the commerce on the river—the old steamboat juxtaposed with the modern vessels carrying cargo up and down the river.

This sternwheeler travels from the dock at the Toulouse Street Wharf three times each day. The *Natchez* is a unique place to eat while you are in the city. Enjoying the view of the river, traveling the way gamblers and merchants did so many years ago is an experience that should not be missed. The food on the *Natchez* is very traditional, as it should be. The meals are served buffet style, giving you lots of opportunities to try traditional dishes such as red beans and rice, fried chicken, gumbo, bread pudding, and more. There are carving stations and lots of changing side dishes. Depending on the time of your trip, you might have live music by the Grammy-nominated Dukes of Dixieland, which makes the dining experience even more enjoyable.

Drinks and wine are available. The cocktail program is not cutting edge, but the classic cocktails are available. Dining or brunching, the experience on the river makes you imagine the young Mark Twain traveling up and down these very waters. Landing at the dock in the French Quarter puts you right in the heart of the old city. This is as much a cultural experience as it is a dining experience.

Top: The dinner cruise.

Bottom: Music on board the dinner cruise.

Toulouse Street Wharf
New Orleans, LA
800-233-2628

CREOLE CREAMERY

The taste of New Orleans is cold and sweet

This eatery is all about ice cream. Not only are the flavors innovative and interesting, but there is an underlying attitude of largesse that encourages excess. For example, there is a sundae called the Tchoupitoulas named after the street by that name. The Tchoupitoulas is so large—as large as its name, if you will—that if you finish it unaided, your name will be immortalized on their hall-of-fame plaque. David Bergeron, founder of Creole Creamery, created this eight-scoop/eight-topping sundae as a family treat to be shared. But those brave souls who manage to eat all of the ice cream are so proud that they deserve to be honored. This massive dessert challenge has been featured on at least three Food Network shows. The Uptown location occupies the site of the old McKenzie's Bakery, which was famous for its traditional king cake. Bergeron and his co-founder Bryan Gilmore, have continued to provide traditional treats, and people have been flocking there since it opened its doors in 2004.

Besides scoops and scoops of ice cream, you can order a banana split, milkshake, float, malt, or other ice cream concoction. There is even an ice cream called the Susie Q that is made without sugar. You can't even find an excuse not to eat at this place. And the very reasonably priced sampler of four mini-scoops helps those of us who cannot make a choice. One flavor is nectar. New Orleans claims this flavor as its own—a merger of vanilla and almond with color from grenadine, often called nectar soda. It makes a mighty fine ice cream.

There are always changing flavors, but there are a few flavors you can count on like vanilla, chocolate, and maybe Creole cream cheese. If you

There are two locations of Creole Creamery, each with its own personality, both serving the same wonderful ice cream.

Left: Banana split.
Right: A float.

can, taste the Creole cream cheese—a sweet and tangy ice cream that is a New Orleans favorite.

Creole cream cheese is a yogurt-like fresh cheese that is only made in the New Orleans area. New Orleans is hot and damp and does not really provide an environment for natural cheeses to age. Through experimentation, early settlers found that by leaving milk out overnight, natural bacteria and yeasts in the air would make a tangy, fermented fresh-milk cheese. It used to be made by local dairies and was eaten by lots of citizens with figs or strawberries in the mornings for breakfast. Sometimes it was spread on French bread. Katz & Besthoff, a now-closed drug store, made ice cream from the cheese. Creole cream cheese ice cream will always be a point of nostalgia for New Orleanians of a certain age.

Uptown
4924 Prytania St.
New Orleans, LA
504-894-8680

Lakeview
6260 Vicksburg St.
New Orleans, LA
504-482-2924

creolecreamery.com

CAFÉ RECONCILE

Doing good and eating well

Only open for lunch and located on the Oretha Castle Haley Boulevard corridor, this bright and airy restaurant features food and service that is prepared and served by students who are being trained through the Café Reconcile program. Founded in 1996 by the Rev. Harry Tompson, SJ, along with Craig Cuccia and Tim Falcon, the program seeks to end the generational cycle of poverty among youth in the Central City neighborhood through workforce and life development skills programs. Since its inception, it's helped more than 1500 youths graduate from the program and on to successful futures.

Café Reconcile is the arm of the program that focuses on an arena that has great cultural value in New Orleans—the food industry. Eating at Café Reconcile allows the diner to interact with those students committed to their service rotation, eat the food being produced by the students working in the kitchen, and support the program—all at the same time. The meals served are very affordable and traditional, like red beans and rice, fried fish, fried chicken, gumbo, and jambalaya. It's a busy place, so arrive early or be prepared to wait.

The gumbo is a traditional New Orleans version: chicken, sausage, and okra. When you order it, ask the server to tell you about it. You'll enjoy how proud the young people are of their food, that you are choosing to eat there, and that they have been a part of it. Catfish, which might be covered with crawfish sauce, jerk chicken, and salmon are all part of the choices that Café Reconcile offers.

There is always a vegetarian meal offered. There are po'boys—shrimp, catfish, or boneless chicken—which are traditionally prepared. The daily specials are usually the best choice. The red beans and rice are really good. The Friday special of shrimp and eggplant Jennifer is definitely a good choice.

Top: Third class.

Right: Lunch plate of the day.

The sides include mashed sweet potatoes, smothered greens, macaroni and cheese, French fries, okra, and corn bread. The bananas Foster bread pudding is definitely the pick for dessert. You will be happy with the food and charmed by the servers.

1631 Oretha Castle Haley Blvd.
New Orleans, LA
504-568-1157
cafereconcile.org

COCHON BUTCHER

The place where the house-made preserved meats reside

Cochon, the restaurant, focuses on serving up an incredible bounty of Cajun delicacies while using the whole pig like its French name might imply. Those inspired by these flavors, or who just want a more casual taste, have made its offshoot neighbor into a resounding success as well.

The spot that Cochon Butcher occupies started out a lot smaller than it is now. It's located right next door to its older sibling, Cochon. Originally there was a counter and a few stools where you could order a sandwich or a smoked meat plate. But Cochon Butcher was really a butcher shop where you could buy Cochon-made sausages, hams, and smoked meats. You could also buy their mustard, pickles, jams, jellies, hot sauce, and now other kitchen goodies like enamelware and butcher blocks. But those who recognized a good sandwich were happy to stand in line to order and either eat their sandwich in a nearby park or back at the office.

As they watched its popularity grow, Cochon's owners—Donald Link and the rest of the Link Restaurant Group—took advantage of an opportunity to secure the adjacent building and created an expanded store with much more eating space. One thing that is recommended is the terrine, a succulent and full-flavored pâté served cold. The sandwiches, like the house-made pastrami with sauerkraut on rye or the Chochon muffuletta, which is piled with house-made charcuterie and olive salad, are all worthy of a repeat visit. The Moroccan sandwich

> If you need a special type of gift–something well made and interesting, but not for a precious table–you can shop at the market portion of the Cochon Butcher.

Left: Macaroni and cheese.
Right: The Gambino.

is made with spiced lamb, mint, cucumbers, and tzatziki on a flatbread. Le Pic Mac is a clever nod to its almost namesake, "Two all *pork* patties, special sauce, lettuce, cheese, pickle, onion, on a sesame bun."

The sliders are great fun, especially to have with a beer, cocktails, or a glass of wine. The pimento cheese slider is unexpected and delicious and the duck pastrami slider is really a good choice. Adventurous diners might be inspired to try head cheese with chow chow: a terrine made with the meat of the hog's head with the gelatin from the pig's bones. The charcuterie plate and the cheese plate can be shared.

There are dinner specials each night. The red beans and rice, the traditional Monday dish, is served with a pork chop. The Thursday special is a boudin-stuffed chicken leg. The Friday fish fry is always a good choice, as is the Saturday fried chicken and watermelon special. There are cookies and brownies for dessert. And for the especially decadent moment, the bacon praline is a good choice. There are also slices of cake from its sister restaurant, La Boulangerie. Wine is available by the glass and bottle, and the cocktail menu is fun and delicious.

930 Tchoupitoulas St.
New Orleans, LA
504-588-7675
cochonbutcher.com

PARKWAY BAKERY AND TAVERN

The poor boy restaurant to the President

Parkway Bakery and Tavern opened in 1911. It has been serving up poor boys since poor boys were invented. It was Jay Nix who reopened Parkway after it had been empty and dormant for years. And what he did was diligently recreate a neighborhood hub. Today Parkway Bakery and Tavern is a neighborhood anchor and a delicious attraction for people from outside of the neighborhood.

Jay Nix is very aware of the origin story of the poor boy. The story tells us that the Martin Brothers (Bennie and Clovis), who were once streetcar workers, left that work and became owners of Martin Brothers Bakery and Coffee Shop. During a very violent streetcar worker strike in 1929, the strikers were hungry. In sympathy for the plight of the strikers, the Martin Brothers gave them gravy sandwiches (some versions of the story say potato sandwiches). Later, one of the Martin brothers asked for people who supported the strikers to help those "poor boys" on the picket line by donating food. Based on that appeal, the Martin Brothers Bakery received help in providing sandwiches for the struggling strikers, thus the sandwiches became known as "poor boys." Then owner of Parkway, Henry Timothy, added the name Poor Boy to the Parkway name as a way to support the workers.

In 1978 a flood destroyed the original ovens that had been installed in the shop. The Timothy family, who had been selling poor boys, now turned to Leidenheimer's Bakery to buy the bread for their poor boy sandwiches. In 1988 the American Can Company closed, which meant that the workers who ate a poor boy every day were no longer around, drying up demand and ultimately leading to the closing of Parkway Bakery just five years later. Shortly thereafter, Jay Nix bought

Roast beef poor boy.
Credit: Tammie Quintana
for Parkway Bakery and
Tavern.

the building, reopening Parkway in 2005 using his own family's roast beef recipe to create a tasty roast beef poor boy. He's opted to maintain the historic name for the sandwich, rather than shortening it to the more popular "po-boy" or even "po'boy," and has taken pains to ensure the preservation of the original, "poor boy." It's an homage to the 1929 strikers who made the sandwich famous during hard times.

The menu at Parkway is not complicated. There is the roast beef poor boy. There are a handful of fried seafood sandwiches. There are sausage poor boys and hamburger poor boys. There's a hot dog poor boy and a few vegetarian options and Reuben poor boy. But having said that, you can find endless variations in your particular order. You may want roast beef gravy on your fried oyster poor boy. You may want chili on your hot sausage poor boy. In other words, no matter how simple the menu is, there are infinite possibilities for personal variation.

Desserts include rum cake, banana pudding (ordered by President Obama), and bread pudding. Everything is freshly made at Parkway. And let us not forget that Parkway is also a tavern, meaning it serves cocktails and beer as well as a limited wine list. There's a special menu for bar snacks.

538 Hagan Ave.
New Orleans, LA
504-482-3047
parkwaypoorboys.com

RESTAURANTS A TO Z

1000 Figs, 20
3141 Ponce de Leon St.

American Sector Restaurant & Bar, 66
1035 Magazine St.

Andrea's, 36
3100 19th St.

Angelo Brocato Original Italian Ice Cream Parlor, 124
214 N. Carrollton Ave.

Antoine's, 114
713 St. Louis St.

Arnaud's, 10
813 Bienville St.

Atomic Burger, 136
3934 Veterans Blvd.

Avo, 74
5909 Magazine St.

Bayona, 16
430 Dauphine St.

Beachbum Berry's Latitude 29, 144
321 N. Peters St.

Between the Bread, 4
625 St. Charles Ave.

Bistro Orleans, 172
3216 W. Esplanade Ave.

Blue Oak Barbecue, 50
900 N. Carrollton Ave.

Bon Ton Café, 164
401 Magazine St.

Bourbon House, 56
144 Bourbon St.

Brennan's, 30
417 Royal St.

Broussard's, 122
819 Conti St.

Bywater American Bistro, 160
2900 Chartres St.

Café at the Square, 46
500 St. Charles Ave.

Café Beignet, 64
311 Bourbon St.
334 Royal St.
600 Decatur St.

Café Conti, 134
830 Conti St.

Café Degas, 170
3127 Esplanade Ave.

Café du Monde, 80
800 Decatur St.

Café Reconcile, 186
1631 Oretha Castle Haley Blvd.

Carmo, 54
527 Julia St.

Carrollton Market, 6
8132 Hampson St.

Casa Borrega, 142
1719 Oretha Castle Haley Blvd.

Central Grocery, 158
923 Decatur St.

Charlie's Steakhouse and Bar, 72
4510 Dryades St.

Cochon, 28
930 Tchoupitoulas St.

Cochon Butcher, 188
930 Tchoupitoulas St.

Commander's Palace, 82
1403 Washington Ave.

Compère Lapin, 180
535 Tchoupitoulas St.

Coquette, 138
2800 Magazine St.

Creole Creamery, 184
4924 Prytania St.
6260 Vicksburg St.

Cure, 38
4905 Freret St.

Dakota, 152
629 N. Hwy. 190

**Dickie Brennan's
Steakhouse, 104**
716 Iberville St.

**Dooky Chase's
Restaurant, 112**
2301 Orleans Ave.

**Drago's Seafood
Restaurant, 44**
3232 N. Arnoult Rd.
2 Poydras St.

DTB, 52
8201 Oak St.

EAT New Orleans, 70
900 Dumaine St.

Five Happiness, 174
3605 S. Carrollton Ave.

Galatoire's, 140
209 Bourbon St.

**The Grill Room at Windsor
Court, 62**
300 Gravier St.

GW Fins, 42
808 Bienville St.

Heard Dat Kitchen, 132
2520 Felicity St.

**Herbsaint Bar and
Restaurant, 120**
701 St. Charles Ave.

Jacques-Imo's, 2
8324 Oak St.

Kin, 146
4600 Washington Ave.

K-Paul's Louisiana Kitchen, 116
416 Chartres St.

La Boulangerie, 84
4600 Magazine St.

**Le Croissant d'Or
Patisserie, 18**
617 Ursulines St.

Luvi, 68
5236 Tchoupitoulas St.

Maypop, 22
611 O'Keefe Ave.

Mondo, 76
900 Harrison Ave.

MoPho, 162
514 City Park Ave.

Mosquito Supper Club, 126
3824 Dryades St.

Napoleon House, 106
500 Chartres St.

Palace Café, 178
605 Canal St.

**Parkway Bakery and
Tavern, 190**
538 Hagan Ave.

Pêche Seafood Grill, 60
800 Magazine St.

Pizza Delicious, 154
617 Piety St.

Port of Call, 24
838 Esplanade Ave.

Pythian Market, 130
234 Loyola

Ralph's on the Park, 176
900 City Park Ave.

Revel Café & Bar, 108
133 N. Carrollton Ave.

Rocky & Carlo's, 12
613 W. St. Bernard Hwy.

Sac-a-Lait, 168
1051 Annunciation

Salon by Sucré, 40
622 B Conti St. (Upstairs)

SoBou, 166
310 Chartres St.

Steamboat *Natchez*, 182
Toulouse Street Wharf

Stein's Market & Deli, 48
2207 Magazine St.

St. James Cheese Company, 32
5004 Prytania St.
641 Tchoupitoulis St.

St. Roch Market, 148
2381 St. Claude Ave.

Sucré, 156
3025 Magazine St.
622 Conti St.

Tableau, 110
616 St. Peter St.

Tartine New Orleans, 14
7217 Perrier St.

Today's Ketch Seafood, 118
2110 Judge Perez Dr.

Toups' Meatery, 150
845 N. Carrollton Ave.

Toups South, 34
1504 Oretha Castle Haley Blvd.

Tujague's Restaurant, 128
823 Decatur St.

Turkey and the Wolf, 26
739 Jackson Ave.

Upperline, 78
1413 Upperline St.

Vacherie, 58
827 Toulouse St.

Willa Jean, 8
611 O'Keefe St.

ESTABLISHMENTS BY NEIGHBORHOOD